Best Wishes!
Ron Wilkee

NEW ORLEANS
SCRAPBOOK

BY

ROSS YOCKEY

**Plantain
Publishing**

NEW ORLEANS SCRAPBOOK

First Printing 1988.

Published by

PLANTAIN PUBLISHING, INC.
P.O. Box 6434
Metairie, Louisiana 70009

ISBN 0–929199–00–6 cloth
ISBN 0–929199–01–4 paper

A Banana Book

Printed in the United States of America

This book is dedicated to
Lauren Beth Yockey,
My wondrous daughter, teacher, friend.

Photo Montages by Joann Yockey
Cover Illustration by Carol Scott
Additional artwork by Harrell Gray

Note:

It would have been impossible to write this book without using real names, where the characters are real people of the past and present. However, since others depicted here are creatures of the imagination, it was necessary to make up names for them. It is quite possible, even probable that other people lay claim to these same names. There is no helping that. I will just have to take my chances. As for those real people who find themselves stuck forever in these pages, I can only trust that the love I feel for them is returned in sufficient quantity that they can overlook the insult they'll most likely feel.

–The Author

If dreams are the memories of the soul, then New Orleans really is the city of dreamy dreams. Just like the song says.

Laid out like the recollection of some provincial European capital, east bank, west bank. Ghettos where palmettos were, like new weeds grown about the old burial cities. Pagan festivals kept alive. Politician-rulers rapt up in the good old days of *laissez majestée.* Memories and dreams, dreams and memories.

If history's what you want you'll find it square and properly annotated in a hundred books nobody reads. Or go and worship at her uptown altars, the coffee tables of society. This book's like none of those, no more than a scrapbook. Memories and dreams so mixed up, dog-eared and scribbled over it's hard to tell the good from the bad, the wisdom from the wishes.

New Orleans and the romantic New Orleanians have been brave, a valiant people who have built a city on a mudhole and one that is a better place in which to live than most places. Despite all the foolishness and the sins and the caste snobbery they have made it that. It is certainly the American city where you are least likely to be bored.

— *Robert Tallant,*
  Romantic New Orleans, 1950

JUST PALS

to be
bored

NUDE BOY ON ROOFTOP

A hundred million years ago Louisiana was hardly a gleam in God's eye, let alone a beam. The coastline of the North American continent curved up out of west Texas then. The Gulf Coast beaches were in Oklahoma and Arkansas. The Cretaceous coastline did not descend to the region of our modern shore until it reached a point near the present Mississippi-Alabama border.

Dinosaurs grazed around Memphis, but in our neighborhood there was only sea life. Just north of Baton Rouge, billions upon billions of tiny sea creatures lived and died, creating with their skeletons a spectacular coral reef. Layer by layer, over millions of years, this living reef grew to form a barrier against the strong ocean currents. Between the reef and the coastline to the north, the water settled into a sleepy lagoon.

Meanwhile, far inland, chains of mountains were building, hastening the pace of erosion. Rains washed sand and clay into streams. Rivers carried the sediments down to the southern shore, filling up the great lagoon. In an epoch or two, there was a place to put Shreveport, Alexandria, Monroe, and Bastrop. The continent had a new southern plain, sloping gently down to the beaches where the reef used to be. But if the mountain-building had ended then, there would be no New Orleans.

Instead, the process continued. New mineral-rich clay and sand washed down the streams and rivers to the southern shore. Thanks to the coral reef, there was an abrupt drop offshore like an underwater cliff. When the sediments hit land's end they slid over the edge like half-

4

chilled Jell-O slopping over the rim of a bowl. This silt, this organic ooze, lay in pools on the ocean floor until it, too, was covered up. The ooze became oil and natural gas, puddles of petroleum known as the Tuscaloosa Trend.

The land continued building southward until at last Louisiana's boot had a toe and Mississippi got a place to build condominiums.

For all those centuries, the chief depositor in Louisiana's land bank has been the Mississippi River. Always a wanderer, the River made itself first one channel, then another. It was only a peculiar conjunction of earth history and human history that brought the Le Moyne brothers and the River together at the shores of Lake Pontchartrain in 1699 A. D. Another tick of the geological clock, one second either way, and the French might have settled somewhere else.

In the place they named Louisiana, the French found dwindling survivors of a once-great Indian nation, the Chatahs, or Choctaws. The Choctaws understood the unpredictablility of Louisiana's waterways. What today was a *hatcha* (river) might tomorrow be only a *bayuk* (bayou). Or it could work the other way just as easily.

A few miles above the site Bienville chose for his city, the Choctaws recalled, the great River had once split into two channels, both of which flowed to the Gulf. But years earlier, the fickle River had changed its mind, sealed off the eastern channel and left only still water. Nevertheless, the Choctaws continued to call the channel a *hatcha*, not a *bayuk*. Because this *hatcha* was still and could turn to mud in the drier months, it became a breeding ground for the strange fish they called a *shupic*.

You could, and still can, eat a *shupic* if you're really hungry, but the Cajun cookbooks do not contain recipes for them, not even blackened. The French spelled the word "choupique," and so the fish has remained into modern English.

Choupiques date back to the dinosaur era, the sole living species of an entire fish order. They grow to two feet in length, with powerful jaws that can cut a large trout in half with a single snap. The males build nests and care for the young. Choupiques have a peculiar swim bladder that lets them breathe air and they are tough enough to spend a season in soggy mud. In fact, they've been known to settle down in flooded fields, to be plowed up alive after the fields are dry enough to plant. "They are the only fish in the world," writes John Chase, "that can be fished for with a pick and shovel; and they actually have been in Louisiana."

It was because of the great number of choupiques found in the false east fork of the Mississippi that the Choctaws called it *Shupic-Hatcha*. The land pushed up by the former flow of the river formed a natural ridge, which became the high road into the city after the land above New Orleans was settled.

That land belonged at first to Joseph Chauvin De Lery. He was granted a deed in 1719, a year after the establishment of New Orleans. Chauvin parceled out the land to share-croppers, forming what the French called a *metairie* or shared farm. The ridge along the *Shupic-Hatcha* became Metairie Road. Eventually, map-makers threw out the Choctaw influence and downgraded the *hatcha* to a *bayuk*. The once important fork of the Mississippi became Bayou Metairie. There is still a tiny piece of it left, paralleling City Park Avenue in City Park.

A few miles above New Orleans, where once the *Shupic-Hatcha* flowed, where earlier the deep sea churned, and where later the choupiques built their nests, there now

6

stands a small frame house. Today it is painted blue, but once it was white. The house is a weatherboard box on brick piers, like a hundred others on its street, built to contain the families of GIs returning from World War II to begin the baby boom.

On an August day in 1951, a small boy crept out of the back door of this house. He was wearing only his underwear. He shut the door softly behind him and walked barefoot toward the rear of the family garage where a raintree grew. When he reached the raintree, the boy took off his underwear and began to climb the tree, naked.

Why?

Perhaps it was that he already knew the Mowgli stories by heart and had moved on to Borroughs and the *Tarzan* books. Perhaps it was the *Chatah* influence seeping up through the landfill. Perhaps he felt already the need to dislodge himself from the present, to explore the then and the when.

Why?

Who knows.

Dawn was only just breaking and the colors were all shades of gray. He could climb like a monkey. The garage roof was no trick: he'd made the swing from the raintree branch a dozen times before to redeem lost balls and windup airplanes. He saw a ragdoll he'd thrown up the day before in a fight with his sister. Repentant or magnanimous, he kicked it down into the yard. There was a puddle on the flat roof from yesterday afternoon's shower and he splashed in it for good measure. Then, crouched down like a Hollywood Indian scout, he ran toward the front corner of the garage.

It was there the garage came nearest to the rear corner of the house. He'd never been on the roof of the house

7

before.

Looking up, the gap between house and garage seemed puny. Looking down it was a chasm. Bricks set on angles as a garden border were mean spears driven into the ground, to impale him if he fell.

Fear is just a short word for challenge to a seven-year-old boy. He gauged the leap, bent his knees and pushed, landing on all fours on the corrugated asphalt roof of the back porch. Gingerly, staying but a short moment in one place, he picked his way quickly along the ridges and furrows to the sloped roof of the house proper. (His father had added the porch and he had no reason to believe his father knew anything about roof-building.)

Now the going got tough. He'd never even climbed a hill, but instinct told him to lean forward on the roof and grip with his toes. The rippled surface of slate shingles was cool and brittle. His finger caught on a lifted nail and tore, bled. He sucked it.

At the peak, his hands closed around the orange clay ridge tiles. They felt good, of the earth. He pulled himself up and looked around. Like Balboa.

Here was his world from a new vantage point. It was a large world, with the great River on his left, the wide Lake on his right, the city behind him, and the rest of the American continent ahead of him. He could see very little of it, of course, because the house was only one story high and there were tall trees in any direction he looked. Still, it was the best vantage point he'd ever had. He stretched out on the still-cool slate and spread his elbows out over the ridge tiles for support. The sun was coming up.

Out by Bonnabel Boulevard, where the little farmyards began, where the Indian burial mounds puckered up like beaver dams near the edge of the Lake, two roosters crowed.

8

A bus went by on Metairie Road.

Across the street a door opened and Mr. Neumann, the tall, red-headed German came out in his robe and slippers for the newspaper. Mr. Neumann did not seem tall from here, and the boy could see where his hair was going thin on top. From here a grownup could not impose the tyranny of height. Mr. Neumann did not see the boy naked on the rooftop. The boy was invisible. He turned and shuffled inside with his newspaper.

The boy knew he should go too. His family would be stirring. A mocking-bird went off like a string of firecrackers on the telephone pole a few yards away. The boy started, startled. Then he laughed at himself. Everything seemed different up there on the roof.

The street was nearer and narrower than it could have been. Where was the wide front yard that held the afternoon football games and the long rounds of "Mother-May-I" that stretched from the sidewalk to the front door? The thin strip of green between the eaves of the house and the white sidewalk seemed hardly wide enough to mow.

But he dropped the thought. He would feel none of that. He was only seven years old and this was his own wide world. On impulse, he stood, straddling the ridge tiles. Nothing between him and the world, from the Indian mounds to the New Basin Canal to the old forts at the Rigolets and the ferry landing at Jackson Avenue: his world.

He scampered down like a waterskimmer treading on surface tension, leaped to the garage, swung to the tree, slid to the ground, slipped into his underwear, and hustled back into the house before somebody caught him. He was seven years old and he'd climbed his first mountain.

THE INDIAN MOUNDS

Rode our bikes to the Injun mounds.
Tribal dump, burial grounds...
Nobody knew for sure.
Out by the lake, real deep wood,
Lose our way be gone for good.
Kids never stop to think.
Dug around with an oyster shell,
Hit something hard, gave a yell.
Seemed like an arrowhead.
Used it to carve in an old elm tree
Or wild magnolia (same to me)
All our important names.

New worlds build on the backs of old.
Injun mound land's all been sold,
Turned into high-priced homes.
Hang our hammocks on ancient trees,
Feed our lawns on memories,
Azaleas on the bones.
Sidewalk bikes, the boom-box sounds
Roll around the Injun mounds...
Kids never stop to think.
Sooner, later, we'll have our turns.
Mounds or tombs or ash-filled urns.
Nobody knows for sure.

THE LE MOYNE BROTHERS

Rene Robert Cavelier, sieur de La Salle, would have founded New Orleans but he got lost and discovered Texas. There was nothing in Texas but mesquite and armadillo and the barbecue had yet to be invented. La Salle knew Louisiana was somewhere around because he'd named it himself just three years earlier. But this was not the place. There being nothing to keep him in Texas, La Salle set out on foot for Canada, but his men killed him along the way.

So it was not La Salle but the Le Moyne brothers who made New Orleans the fun place it is today.

Charles Le Moyne was a Norman commoner who built a fortune the hard way in Canada. Louis XIV gave him a title. His wife gave him eleven sons, also titled. The oldest Le Moyne son, Pierre, sieur d'Iberville, was selected to lead the second French attempt at colonizing Louisiana. He first succeeded in locating the Mississippi River, which had eluded La Salle, then he opted for a settlement site near what is now Biloxi, Mississippi. Pierre went back to France for more colonists and left his teenage brother Jean, in charge.

Jean Baptiste Le Moyne, sieur de Bienville, could not rid himself of the notion that the place for a settlement was right on the banks of that big muddy river. So in late 1699, while his brother was away, Bienville took one of his ships and sailed up the Mississippi. But for his whim, Louisiana might have been settled by the British. Rather than add chicory to coffee, New Orleanians might be toughening their tea and nibbling on scones instead of beignets. Life for all the world might have been different if Bienville hadn't been born with itchy feet and the ability to lie with a straight face.

11

After sailing up to Baton Rouge and impressing the local Indians, Jean Baptiste came about and headed back downriver toward the Gulf. Just beyond the lower tip of the crescent that gives New Orleans its nickname, the river makes a hairpin bend. Bienville was just rounding that bend when someone spotted another ship sailing upriver. It flew a British flag and looked like a twelve-gun corvette. Bienville figured he could talk his way out of a tough spot. He hailed and pulled alongside the bigger ship to have a word with the captain, who wanted directions to the nearest likely settlement. The English were looking for a place to plant their flag and get the home fires burning. Bienville pointed upriver. "You can't see them, on account of that turn in the river," he said, "but right behind me is a large French settlement and fort. We've been eager to test the cannons."

The English captain, Lewis Banks, asked for directions to Texas, turned his ship around and headed for the Gulf under full sail. To this day that bend in the river beyond which the make-believe fortress lay is known as English Turn.

SIREN SONG OF JOHN LAW

Come sail with me to Paradis
    And claim a piece of Eden there,
Where land is bountiful and free
    And gentle breezes waft the air.
Beside your bride an Indian maid
    With skillful hands and bosom bare
Shall hammock in the palm-tree glade,
    The wealth of Nature yours to share.

Across the sea, to Paradis,
    Where natives stand in line to trade
For missals, rum and beads with thee,
    Their gold and silver, furs and jade.
Oh, can you see in Paradis
    The red tile roofs and white tall spires?
Allons, amis! Believe thee me,
    It's truth they tell who sell with lyres.

MAKE-BELIEVE CITY

It was all make-believe.

Bienville held out for a riverbank settlement and the government of France declared it so. But the boy King Louis XV and his regents had neither time nor temperament for governing a colony many times the size of their own kingdom and half a world away. They decided to award the operation of Louisiana to a private contractor, much the same as large cities today handle their waste disposal.

The first proprietor of Louisiana (which included, of course, the entire central slice of today's United States) was Antoine Crozat, Marquis de Chatel. In five years, from 1712 to 1717, Crozat managed to swell the French population of this vast territory from four hundred to about seven hundred souls. This included at least twenty-five French women. At the end of five years the Marquis was nearly destitute, begging the King to take Louisiana off his hands.

Enter John Law and the Company of the West, later the Company of the Indies.

Law, was a somewhat lawless Scot, a professional gambler who fled Scotland after killing the husband of his lover in a duel. Just the man to run Louisiana. Law issued bank notes based on anticipated revenues which would pour in from Louisiana. This "Mississippi Bubble" lasted three years before it burst and Law was blown out of yet another country.

But John Law was an intrepid promoter. He papered France with slick leaflets and posters illustrating the milk and honey, the golden opportunity awaiting French entrepreneurs in the thriving American colony. His poster *Le*

Commerce que les Indiens du Mexique font avec les Francois au Port de Missisipi is a masterpiece of deceptive advertising. In the foreground rum-swilling, Bible-toting, bare-breasted Indians relinquish all their worldly possessions to glad-handling Frenchmen. In the distance, below the gentle mountain peaks of New Orleans is the outline of a fair metropolis where "the soil need only be tickled to yield up either a smiling harvest or bountiful gold."

Law, whom Mel Leavitt calls "one of history's grand connivers," never succeeded in his goal of transplanting six thousand willing French colonists a year. Hardly anyone bought the promise of a rose garden. The government agreed to open up the prison doors to any lawbreaker who'd go to the colony. They stayed in jail. Finally convicts and vagrants were dragged forcibly from their cells and gutters to populate Louisiana. Beggars, prostitutes, drunkards, gamblers, thieves, and cutthroats — these were the pilgrims of New Orleans' Mayflowers.

To the government's apparent surprise, these colonists brought their old lifestyles with them. They instituted a drinking, gambling, whoring, idling *joie de vivre* that has endured infusions of Irish, Germans, Yankees, and even Protestants. The very slaves imported from Africa and the West Indies were Gallicized. We're all French under the skin.

How strange the name New Orleans sounds to us, in the southern states of America. As if our daughter is to travel to the lands of the Indies, we think it no less far.

— *Lillian Hellman,*
  Pentimento, 1973

A NUN'S TALE

On February 23, 1727, thirteen Ursuline nuns set sail aboard *La Gironde* from l'Orient, France, for New Orleans. Their aim was to establish the colony's first convent and first school. Despite horrendous storms, deathbed bouts of *mal de mer*, the attentions of no fewer than five pirate ships and running aground twice, *La Gironde* and its precious cargo made it to Louisiana. The Ursulines arrived in New Orleans on the eighth of August 1727, and their influence was immediate. But for these Ursulines, it is doubtful the Lord would have permitted the city's survival into the nineteenth century.

One of the nuns, Marie-Madeleine Hachard, Sister St. Stanislaus, wrote five letters to her father in Rouen during the first year of her service in the colony. The father had them printed locally. In 1971 a New Orleanian, Myldred Masson Costa, dug up a copy of the letters in the *Archives de Rouen* and, several years later she managed to have her translation printed up in a little gem of a book. It should be included in every Louisiana history class, but it isn't.

Marie-Madeleine was twenty-three when she wrote her father, wide-eyed at her new surroundings and awed by her own sense of purpose. Her letters tremble with intimidation at the dark forests of strange towering trees, crowding each other to drink from the wide, wide river. Cane twenty feet high and wild rice, alligators and "an infinity of fish which are unknown in France" greet the provincial Europeans as they tack and row upriver. Murderous torrents of *maringouins* (mosquitos) welcome them to the New World. Eggs are fifty sols a dozen, and one pays twice the price for only

17

half the amount of milk sold in Rouen. She tries not to complain about the food, but the distaste comes through when she mentions *sagamite.* Her recipe calls for boiling ground Indian corn meal in water seasoned with bacon fat. Sounds a lot like hominy grits.

Sister St. Stanislaus writes with propriety and with the delicacy required of a religious communicating to her family far away. Still, she cannot hide her displeasure at the morals and pretense she witnesses in her new home. In her first letter from New Orleans she writes:

> *While I do not yet know the country of Louisiana perfectly, I shall however, my dear father, give you a few details. I can assure you that I hardly believe I am at the Mississippi; there is as much politeness and magnificence here as in France and the use of cloth-of-gold and velvet is very common, even though it is three times as expensive as in Rouen.*

> *I shall not speak to you, my dear father, of the morals of the lay people of this country. I do not know them very well and have no desire to meet them, but it is said that they are quite corrupt and scandalous. There are also a great number of honest folks. One does not see any of these girls who were said to have been deported here; none seems to have come as far as this.*

Six months later, Marie-Madeleine at last has made the acquaintance of "these girls." She deplores the local Indian women who "under a modest air hide the passions of beasts." Yet she holds out some hope, however faint, for the French female inhabitants of New Orleans.

18

While the women ignore facts pertaining to their salvation, they ignore nothing when it comes to vanity. The luxury in this city is such that one can distinguish no one; everyone is of equal magnificence.

Most of the women and their families are reduced to living on sagamite, a sort of gruel. However, notwithstanding the expense, they are dressed in velvets and damasks covered with ribbons, materials which are regularly sold in this country for ten times their cost in France. And women here, as elsewhere, use red and white paint and patches, too, to cover the wrinkles in their faces. The devil here possesses a large empire, but this does not discourage us from the hope of destroying him, with God's love.

Marie-Madeleine's hopes are dashed on the rocks of time. Today there are these same women — and men, too — in New Orleans. They paint their faces and deck themselves in gilded gaudery to ride on floats through the streets, dispensing trinkets to be ground underfoot with beer cans and burger bags. Most of them pay not a cent of property tax for public education. Their trinkets and costumes, their cloth-of-gold and velvet, cost millions of dollars each year.

The city has a damned good time.

HOW TO SAY N. O.

The first thing to know about N. O.
Is not to say it wrong.
Don't rhyme it with queens or red beans
Or know-what-it means
Like they do in every song.

If you want folks to think you're from N. O.
Forget what Frenchmen say.
They come to Nouvelle Orleans
To have a bon temps
While they sip on their Perrier.

Now we welcome any call-ins,
Fall-ins or crawl-ins
Who know the right way
Of pronouncing New Orleans;
But say Or-lay-AWNH or New Or-LEENS
And we'll laugh you out of Chez Helene's
(Unless you live on Orleans Street, Bub,
Or meet the girls at the Orleans Club.)

Tell you what.
Fill your mouth with mabbles,
Give your jaw the wobbles
And I'll teach you how it's done
In two to four syllables.

In the proper parlez-ance of certain hip historians,
All but speaking-poorly ones
Pronounce the place "New OAR-l'yuns."
New OAR-l'yuns breaks nobody's rule.
And that's cool.

You can also be a local star
Pronouncing "Or" as "Are,"
And it's not against the law
To change your "Or" to "Awe."
"New ARE-lins" or "New AWE-luns," either way.
That's okay.

But if ya conjugate at Smitty's
Or at Bubba's in St. Bunawd,
If y'a seafood gint or plain half-pint
In some jint in the lower Nint Wawd,
Lemme lay it out straight:
Ay-BREE-vee-ate.
Dat whole ting's too long an too hawd.
Drop dat "Ooo," all yawl dawlins,
An jus say it "N'AW-lins."
Ya got it?
Dat's over, tank Gawd.

"Maringouin perdi so temps quand li piqué caiman."

"Mosquito wastes his time when he stings the gator."

— Creole proverb

Plenty of Creoles about

KING CREOLE

Here we are in the etymological capital of the USA. We've got more misunderstood words per capita than any other town in the universe. Misunderstood by outsiders that is. Try "banquette" on a lad from Cincinnati. Try "mirliton" in Memphis. Of course, most of our odd words at least mean the same things to all of us who use them. Not so with the word "creole."

Though it is a belief some of us would die for, "creole" did not originate in New Orleans. It was around for at least a hundred years before the city began, probably the coinage of some Portuguese sea captain. In Portuguese the word is "crioulo," changed to "criollo" in Spanish, thence to the French "creole." The root is the Latin "creare," which means "to create" or, more germanely, "to beget."

Only in New Orleans, so far as I can tell, has "creole" spawned racial animosity. White folks here want exclusive rights to the word, for white descendants of French and/or Spanish colonials. Blacks demand sole proprietorship for persons of "cafe au lait" complexion. All of us confuse the issue by applying it to tomatoes, okra, gumbo, et cetera, with callous disregard for coloration.

We err only in our jealousy. For more than three hundred years, "creole" has meant all those things and more.

In 1604 D'Acosta's *History of the West Indies* used the word *crollos* for "Spaniards borne at the Indies." The 1748 chronicle of the *Earthquake of Peru* stated that *"Criollo* signifies one born in the Country (Peru); a word made by the Negroes, who give it to their own children born in these Parts." *Juan & Ulloa's Voyages,* published from 1760 to 1772,

24

has it both ways. "The Whites may be divided into two classes, the Europeans and Creoles, or Whites born in the Country," and later, "the class of Negroes is... again subdivided into Creoles and Bozares."

In those days, whatever or whoever traveled from the far side of the Atlantic to this side, set down roots and propagated, its second and later generations were called "creoles."

In New Orleans the word became an adjective as well as a noun. After Napoleon sold the colony to Thomas Jefferson and the Yankee invasion began, anything which could be identified as "creole" was considered superior by the natives. Creole goods brought higher prices. This included slaves as well as produce and livestock, lap quilts and lace.

But step back in time to the earliest days of the city.

The dalliance of masters with slaves was not invented here, but it flourished in New Orleans' fetid climate. The taking of mistresses and lovers was a natural indulgence for New Orleanians, always eager to emulate the aristocracy of France. Here they called it p*laçage.* The Creoles laid into miscegenation with lusty abandon. Soon there were scores of little brown children underfoot. Usually they were awarded "Free Person of Color" status, either out of kindness or guilt, by their white fathers. They grew up and were allowed to make their own way in the world. For many of the girls, being *placée* (placed) as a white man's mistress seemed a noble calling with excellent fringe benefits. The cottage industry thus begotten flourished for generations on the edge of the old city, unlike anything before or since in the United States.

As they removed themselves further and further from slavery, the subsequent generations of "Free People of

Color" could, if they wished, consider themselves superior to those of unbroken African lineage. Since "creole" already meant "better," it was easily adopted by those of mixed race.

The Yankee invasion of the mid-nineteenth century brought its scourge of travel editors and newspaper correspondents. It was they who popularized the belief that a Louisiana Creole was a person of mixed race. White Creoles were enraged and for a century their own writers have been fussing about trying to set the record straight.

In 1872 *Creole State* was suggested as the official nickname of Louisiana. But, as H. L. Mencken observed, that movement died "when ignorant Northerners began assuming that the term connoted African blood." So we are the *Pelican State*. In the 1970s we had to import brown pelicans from Florida just to live up to our name. There were still plenty of Creoles about. Fortunately, the pelicans reproduced, so that these new generations may be called, justifiably, "creole brown pelicans."

Etymologically speaking, there are precious few of us here who couldn't be called "Creoles." Even if we throw in European ancestry as a requisite, many, if not most New Orleans blacks could uncover a Spaniard or Frenchman somewhere back in the family woodpile.

But this argument won't satisfy either side. It's tempests like this that make our gumbo pot so spicy (to stir up the metaphors). Here's the proper chauvinist attitude, as expressed in 1926 by Lyle Saxon in the *Times-Picayune*: "The Creole is one who is born away from his country, whatever his country may be." Only some countries didn't count. "The reason why the word creole has been so often misunderstood is that their (white creoles') slaves spoke a *creole* dialect, bearing about the same relation to pure French as our Southern Negro talk does to English purely spoken."

That argument settled it all for etymologist H. L. Mencken, despite the justifiable claim to Creole-hood by thousands of non-white New Orleanians. In *The American Language* Mencken held "creole" in high esteem, while listing "cajun" as a term of abuse. "The word (cajun) carries a derogatory significance and is never applied to the high-toned French of New Orleans, who are *creoles*. The common — and resented — American assumption that *creole* connotes Negro blood is repeated, in turn, by many Cajuns."

Leave it to the Cajuns, who invented dirty rice and the habit of eating mudbugs, to sully the waters. My maternal grandmother, a white creole lady of wide-ranging and bountiful prejudices, never, to my knowledge, applied the word "creole" to a black person. ("Darky" was her term of affectionate abuse.) But I do recall her once describing a certain, socially acceptable branch of the LeBlanc family as "creole Cajuns." My grandmother had a big creole heart.

LISTEN TO THE MUSIC

Grow up in a city walled with mirrors and it's easy to think the world's watching your every move. Every once in a while Popes and Super Bowls and hurricanes come along to crack the mirrors and give outsiders a peek. That only keeps us believing that everyone out there is just fascinated by what goes on in here. Become a frog of some local repute and you don't doubt for a minute you'll be recognized in the pond *du mond*.

Case in point No. 1:

In the late 60's, just five years out of college, a would-be writer achieves New Orleans stardom as a TV reporter. Gas station attendants and drugstore clerks know his face and cash his checks. He is at the top rung of a short ladder. Seers and peers assure him that he'll have no trouble getting a network job, so he puts his new Aurora Gardens house on the market, sells his car, loans out his drums, and leaves for New York City.

Case in point No. 2:

In the late 60's, just five years out of college, a lovely young singer is the brightest new star on the local classical music scene. She's done the secondary roles with the New Orleans Opera, managed the National Anthem at the Sugar Bowl two years in a row and settled into a teaching career because nobody will pay her to sing in New Orleans. All of a sudden a hotshot tenor named Placido Domingo hears her, tells her she owes it to the world to move to New York, where the coaches and the companies and the agents are. She packs up the china and crystal wedding presents, trades her old spinet for one last month of local vocal lessons, and leaves for New York City.

No. 1 and No. 2 are married. They are naive to the brink of disbelief.

A year later No. 1 is still trying to write his way into a reporter's job at a New York independent TV station. No. 2 is working on her first big role at the Juilliard School (school, not paid) and they know a lot more about small ponds and big ponds and tricks with mirrors.

Flashback:

One of her last big appearances in New Orleans was with the Symphony Orchestra, in the North American premiere of *Escenas Campestras* by Louis Moreau Gottschalk, another native of New Orleans. The first concert they attended after moving to New York was by the American Symphony, Leopold Stokowski conducting. It cost them a dollar each to sit up in the aerie at Carnegie Hall. On the bill was another piece by Louis Moreau Gottschalk. Coincidence?

Flash-forward:

It's 1975 and the big United States Bicentennial is approaching. Both careers are blossoming. Our two cases (still married, *mirabile dictu*) are researching the New York Public Library for a project they can work on together that will wow the world of 1976. Call it fate, call it Kismet, they stumble once again over the almost forgotten body of Louis Moreau Gottschalk's works.

Aside:

Louis Moreau Gottschalk was a wunderkind, the Steven Spielberg of his day. His papa sent him to Paris to study piano and composition in 1842, at the age of thirteen. Louis heard Chopin doing his Polish-folk-music transformations and decided he too could make a living in the Old World by dressing up the folk tunes of the New. So Gottschalk started writing piano pieces based on the music of his childhood, music from New Orleans. His career was made. He was invited to all the best palaces, drank the best wines, ate the best foods. When he returned to the United States in 1853, preceded by his press raves, Louis had no trouble getting bookings all over the country. Gottschalk is a fascinating character, but that's another story.

Back to the point:

If Gottschalk scored so big with this old New Orleans music a hundred years ago, why couldn't our heroine and hero pull off the same trick today? What had become of all this folk music? Why didn't it get played in New Orleans any more? Why did nobody in New Orleans care about Gottschalk?

Why indeed.

It is really surprising that so many people of good taste and refinement should be in the habit of riding in the dirty (street)cars without remonstrating against the monstrous nuisance which has lately crept into those vehicles in the shape of vagabond minstrels and beggarly harpers. These fellows, big and little, force themselves into the cars with ludicrous effrontery, cumber the passage and seats with their huge instruments of discord and chatter away like baboons in the barbarous patois of the Swiss and Italian Alps, until the cars are filled and ready to start. Once in motion, the concert begins — the fiddler saws his catgut, the tambourine is scraped and jangled and thumped, the apology for a harp is thumped and thrummed, whilst a chorus of cracked voices, innocent of all tune, time and harmony, bursts upon the tortured ear, putting to flight all power of thought or conversation.

— New Orleans Daily Crescent
Editorial, June 1, 1866

STREET FARE

The wandering minstrels earn their keep
Touching the guilt that's gilded deep
In the breasts of the best of society.

Juggling fools, clowns with balloons,
Black boys tapping to whistled tunes
To atone for the sins of sobriety.

Penitent players answering the call,
Mannequin mimes doing nothing at all:
The hairshirted martyrs we've made them.

In foolscap and motley, dregs and dross,
Street entertainers come, bearing our cross.
They'll dog us until we have paid them.

CREOLE SONGS

Slaves got Sundays off. The ones with the wildness still in their souls gathered Sunday afternoons in a place labeled with a whiteman's sneer: *Place Congo*. It's a natural ridge of earth, between the old city limits and where the swamp began. The Indians used it for a playing field. Today we call it Louis Armstrong Park.

The drummers generally got there first to set up, as drummers do. Slapping out random rhythms and talking in small groups, those who understood each other's tribal tongues, Mandinga here, Minah there, Kreal, and Yallof. As the crowd built, the talk all spilled into French. It was a new French, steeped through a few generations of enforced ignorance, refined in desperation's fire. Without real teachers, their ears and tongues led them into the strange, elaborate language. Whatever wasn't needed — pronouns, verb endings, articles — got left behind. All the forms of the first personal pronoun, for example, were summed up in "mo." The only trace of the definite article was the "z" sound stuck by elision on the tops of vowel-starting nouns. *"Les oiseaux"* the birds, became *"zozo",* good for a fledgeling or a flock. Pronounciations were vastly simplified. For instance, if a story-teller wanted to say, "When I was a little bird" — *Quand j'eté un petit oiseau* — he rendered it *"Tan mo 'te ti' zozo."* It was called, as Lyle Saxon correctly observed, *Creole French.* It was a terse, lilting language, full of natural rhythms and rhyme. It was born to be sung.

The quill man sounded the first notes, shrill and piercing

33

enough to make a dog howl in Pirate's Alley. You could hear those bamboo pipes clear to the *Place d' Armes* (Jackson Square) just as today you can stand on the bridge in Armstrong Park and hear that steamboat calliope man jamming his sour notes at the *Natchez* dock.

The black folks heard those quill notes and started running. Men and women and even kids who could sneak away to watch. Calico and indigo, scrapheap finery. They came to sing, came to dance, came to let it go and feel free for a few hours. (Later on there'd be tent meetings and revivals, lodge halls and company picnics. Then there was only the dance in *Place Congo* on Sunday afternoons.)

En bas hé
En bas hé
par en bas yé pélélé mo

Goin down, goin down
where that music's beckonin nigh,
with fingers wound round my soul,
Counjaille!

yé pélélé counjaille,
a debautché

It's draggin me down,
the pommelin drum-sound.
That counjaille shame me,
counjaille come to claim me.

It begins thus, slowly, with a *counjaille*. Chanting, some

of the women unwrap their bandanas, their *tignons*, and hold the corners up like the head and tail of a voodoo snake. They sway a wave that starts from deep in the ground and drives up through their feet, legs, thighs, hips, stomachs, breasts, shoulders, arms: *tignon* snake shivers and snaps, offered to the sun. The men moan a pedal point. The drums roll and rumble without a rhythm.

Suddenly a shriek, from low in one woman's throat:

Aieeee... Bamboula! Bam-bou-LA!

A drum breaks off, sets a steady throb. Faster, faster. Other drums jump in. Shouts and claps. Circles form. The *banjar* strums. Gourds rattle and bones. Pipes and whistles play counterpoint. The hard-packed field shakes with the bamboula.

Tan patate-la tchuite, na manja-li, na manja-li.
Tan patate-la tchuite, na manja-li, na manja-li.

What does it mean? Nonsense. Nonsense or wisdom.

When that sweet potato's done, don't you eat it.

Good advice. Better open a yam's jacket and let it cool before you dig in.

The Creole Songs, the ones still around, are full of such sage silliness.

There's topical satire:

Monsieur Preval gave a fancy-dress ball,
Put blacks and whites in a horse's stall.
Made the white folks pay just to dance and play,
Till the sheriff came and shut down that game.

There is heartbreak:

Oh, Zelim, since they sold you away,
I sob all night, I cry all day.

There is pleasure:

Tried every girl up and down the coast,
Still love my Belle Layotte the most.

The lyrics of the Creole songs are probably the richest source of folklore in the United States. The music of the Creole Songs is the cauldron out of which *jazz* would emerge. Hardly anyone in the world today is aware of their existence. Except for the name of next year's Rex, the Creole Songs are New Orleans' best-kept secret.

ZELIM, TO QUITEE LA PLAINE

When we dreamed of life together,
Of the love we two would share,
Every care seemed like a feather
That would vanish in the air.

> *Like leaves, my dreams were scattered*
> *When you left me here alone.*
> *You are gone and love lies shattered*
> *Like a mirror by a stone.*

My Zelim, have you forsaken
All the vows you swore to me?
Was my heart so long mistaken,
Were my eyes too blind to see?

> *These tears, how I have cried them.*
> *Day and night I seem to weep.*
> *As I work I cannot hide them,*
> *Cannot lose them in my sleep.*

Oh, my love, I'm lost without you,
Like a deer lost in the cane.
Never thought that I should doubt you,
Never thought you'd leave again.

> *Each night I walk the levee,*
> *Keeping watch until the dawn.*
> *But my heart grows hard and heavy,*
> *And the river rushes on.*

37

TAN PATATE-LA TCHUITE

That sweet potato's done, but it's too hot,
Yes, it's too hot.
Don't take it from that pot, you better not,
You better not.

> *Don't take it from that pan.*
> *You'll be a sorry man.*
> *Sure gonna burn your han'.*
> *'Cause it's too hot, 'cause it's too hot.*

Though she is very young, she shakes a lot,
She's really hot.
One kiss and you'll be stung by what she's got.
You better not!

> *Lips that are cherry red.*
> *Hips that'll turn your head.*
> *Slip and you'll land in bed.*
> *You better not. You better not.*

Just watch that fellow dance, look at him trot,
Look at him trot.
A man who can romance when he gets hot,
When he gets hot.

> *Look at that old man go,*
> *Thinkin' his wife won't know,*
> *Thinkin' she's pure as snow.*

I think she's not, I think she's not.

You stand before that priest to tie the knot,
To tie the knot.
In church, to say the least, you're on the spot,
You kneel a lot.

You're in a saintly state,
Thinkin' that you'll go straight
Up to that Pearly Gate,
But you might not, you might get hot!

ONCE I MET A LITTLE MAN

Once I met a little man,
Puffing down the road he ran.
Hair so white, his face so black,
Heavy sack upon his back.
"Wait," said I, " I'll help you along."
"Thanks," said he, "but I am strong."

From his sack he pulled a cat,
Saying, "Look, no time to chat."
"Sir," said I, "your clock's a cat,
Can you tell the time with that?"
"No," said he, "but I've got a hunch,
Now's the time to have some lunch."

From the sack came food galore,
Hams and yams and jams and more,
Melons ripe and plaintains brown.
"Now," said he, "to wash it down.
Brandy's sweet, molasses is too,
What you drink is up to you."

I said, "Sir, have you the time?"
He said, "Yes, and that's a crime,
Time is never long enough

To enjoy a pinch of snuff.
Fine tobacco's good for the brain,
Brandy, too, and sugar cane."

"Why," said I, "with time so late
Must you tote a sack so great?"
"Great," said he, "must be indeed,
Just to hold the food I need.
Food it takes to strengthen my back
So that I may tote my sack."

Then once more he took his load,
Went off puffing down the road.
But before he left to stay,
Back he came again to say:
  "Brandy's sweet, molasses is too.
What you drink is up to you."

Should you ever chance to meet
Such a man upon the street,
Say I've shared his thoughts with you,
And beware, for they are true!
"Brandy's sweet, molasses is too,
What you drink is up to you."

MISTER BANJO

Looka little yalla-skin go,
*   Mister Banjo,*
Look at 'im strut his stuff.
Playin like he's white as the snow,
*   Mister Banjo,*
Comical sight, sure nuff.

Straightnin out all his curls,
*   Mister Banjo,*
Winkin at blue-eyed girls.
Takin a bath each day,
*   Mister Banjo,*
Washin that black away!

Watch 'im how he straddles that fence
*   Mister Banjo,*
Eyein them white folks' yards.
Yalla-skin be missin some sense,
*   Mister Banjo,*
Playin with half his cards.

Hopin we'll all forget,
*   Mister Banjo,*
Hopin he'll fool us yet.
Take a lot more than hope,
*   Mister Banjo,*
Take a lot more than soap.

The veritable Congo dance, with its extraordinary rhythmic chant, will soon become as completely forgotten in Louisiana as the signification of those African words which formed the hieratic vocabulary of the voodoos.

— *Lafcadio Hearn,*
"The Scenes of Cable's Romances," Century Magazine, 1883

Symphony Concert
To Mark Gottschalk
Centennial Year

The Centennial Year of the death of Louis Moreau Gottschalk, native of New Orleans who... american-born musician, Chalmette,... national fame, with... New Orleans... orchestra in a ...5 at 8:30 ...The pro-... Torka-... Amer-

Ruins of General Packenham's Home Chalmette, La. New Orleans.

...com-
...and exotic
...ned audiences all
...e died at the age of 40
...ro in 1869.

...chalk works on Tuesday's program ...lude "Escenas Campestres," ...a one act ... which... feature son... Jo Ann Y..., baritone Earl ...edding and te... Randall Veazey; "Montevideo," ...n imposing one movement symphony th... G...chalk composed as a tribut... ...Uruguay, and ...ill perform ...lla" and ...ional

GENERAL SOCIETY OF THE WAR OF 1812
FOUNDED SEPTEMBER 14, 1814

National #
State #
At-Larg...
Date El...

...Y, ROSS PAUL...
...039 Calhoun Street,
...New Orleans, La.

...mpatriot,

Kindly be advised that I have approved and filed y...
accredited member of this society.

...tor....DON FRANCISCO BONAVENTURA Y ALMENTE.....
......Great, Great, Great Grandson......
...Relationship.....La. Volunteers......

...Y General

WAR STORIES

New Orleans is almost completely surrounded by forts. Today they guard only the past, serving as therebys on which tales might be hung.

The first two forts were built by Iberville around 1700. They were nothing but simple, highly pregnable breastworks of earth and timber. They were the meagerest protection for garrisons stationed there to keep English and Spanish ships from sailing up the French river. Later on the French built more forts near the city. So did the Spanish and the British, just to be on the safe side. Mostly these forts sat and waited for glory days that never came, to be eroded by time and battered away by hurricane winds.

When General Andrew Jackson arrived in New Orleans in 1814, he realized the city's fate might well depend on these old, already dilapidated fortresses. New Orleans was about to be attacked by the British, and Jackson put his engineers to work on what he considered the most vulnerable points. Northeast of the city, they reinforced Fort Coquille and Fort Chef Menteur. On the Plaquemines Bend of the river, they improved the old Spanish Fort San Felipe.

A minor footnote to history is that, on the eve of the attack by General Packenham, Jackson sent the author's great, great, great grandfather to defend the indefensible Rigolets Pass, through which an armada could sail unchallenged from the Gulf into Lake Pontchartrain. In his letter to my ancestor, Don Francisco Bonaventure de Alpuente, General Jackson expressed "the forlorn hope" that Alpuente's volunteers could hold the pass if the British chose that route.

Fortunately, Packenham bypassed the Rigolets and moved from Lake Borgne into Bayou Bienvenue. From there he marched to Chalmette and his ill-fated rendezvous with Andy Jackson and Jean Lafitte's pirates. As Stanley Clisby Arthur wrote in *Old Families of Louisiana*, "the historic battle was fought without giving Captain Alpuente the opportunity of taking his men into action to participate in that wonderful and glorious victory."

This unhappy circumstance did not prevent my brother, many years later, from commissioning a replica of the Captain's red-sashed uniform so that he might parade around in high style at the January ball of the Society of the War of 1812 in the State of Louisiana. Of course, my brother Jim was better fortified with scotch whiskey than our ancestor had been with breastworks.

When General Jackson returned to Washington, he crusaded for better defenses around New Orleans and spearheaded the drive to build the Monroe Fortress System. Its forts — Pike, Macomb, Jackson, St. Philip, Proctor and Livingston, Battery Bienvenue and Martello Castle— were obsolete almost from the time they were finished.

In their day, though they impressed. Polygonal outworks, bastions, demibastions, covered ways, crescent batteries. Built mostly of brick and earth on spongy soil, leaning every one of them into the water. Built by slaves and paid laborers and the U. S. Army's best engineers. By 1835 they were complete and manned. For most of them the only attacks would come from yellow fever, malaria, and the howl of hurricanes at summer's end.

Serving for long periods in those dank forts was dull. Water seeped down through walls and up through floors. Sun baked relentlessly. There was drilling all day long, drilling to the din of snare on skin and the rattle of boots on dry clamshells. By night the mosquitos drilled. The men learned somehow to sleep, outside the walls in wooden barracks. Mornings they woke to the hollow stutter of lips caressing brass. Sounds hung in the humid air, lingered like fear, like death. Soldiers grew old waiting to die. Lying too long in their watery soil, the very walls developed bedsores. Even the outbreak of the War Between the States, the Civil War, barely woke them.

Elsewhere those days there was frenzy. Stoves and churchbells were melted down for cannon in Virginia. Mississippi beat its plowshares into swords. New Orleans slept within its impregnable Monroe Fortress System. No one would dare attack.

And then came the steam engine...

April 1862. Flag Officer David Farragut steams up the river toward Plaquemines Bend, bent on breaking the central link in the Confederacy's supply chain. Forts Jackson and St. Philip are ready for him.

General P. G. T. Beauregard has blocked the river with eleven schooner hulks chained together, a floating barricade. Farragut fires from a distance, but after five days and nights of continuous shelling, Jackson and St. Philip appear unscathed. Farragut's only hope is to pass the forts under full steam and full fire. Sailing vessels would not have had a prayer.

Farragut starts around the bend at 2 a. m. April 24. The next three and a half hours will be what historian Charles L. Dufour calls the most awesome naval-land battle of all time. Officers and men on both sides would write their memoirs:

Combine all that you have heard of thunder, add to it all that you have ever seen of lightning and you have, perhaps, a conception of the scene.

47

It was as if the artillery of heaven were playing on the earth.

The crash of splinters, the explosion of the boilers and the magazines, the shouts and cries, the shrieks of scalded and drowning men; add to this the belching flashes of guns, blazing rafts of burning steamboats, the river full of fire, and you have a picture of the battle that was all confined to Plaquemines Bend.

A confederate tug shoves a burning barge under the bow of the *Hartford*, the Union flagship. "My God," screams Farragut as his ship bursts into flames, "is it to end this way?" He regains control. "Don't flinch from that fire, boys! There is a hotter fire than that for those who don't do their duty!"

But in the end, the irresistible force pushes past the immovable object. Steam power. The forts are finished.

Fort Jackson, on the west bank, is ruined. Its drawbridge is splinter and ash. Smoke-hazed sunlight streams through wide cracks that run the height of its outer walls. Its passageways are flooded by water rushing through holes in the lower earthworks. It has received the punishment of six thousand shells. Its days, like those of the Confederacy, are numbered.

Today you can tour Fort Jackson, if you don't mind the parochial touches — fluorescent lighting, wrought-iron guardrails, and the like. You can get there on Louisiana Highway 23 across the river.

But I recommend Fort Pike, on the Rigolets, where my great, great, great grandfather and his troops sat out the

Battle of New Orleans. Fort Pike's been left the way it was, out Highway 90 east, within the city limits.

You can be alone there with the sun and the sound of waves lapping against the old bricks. Walk the sodden ramparts and the sullen, dank passageways. Duck the low arches.

You feel it here, that pall of human mistrust, ageless and enduring.

Linger for a while in the cool, deceptive catacombs.

Ponder the religious ecstasy of war.

The story of old New Orleans ends with the Civil War...The period of Reconstruction in Louisiana is the most tragic part of its story. New Orleans had been one of the richest — if not the richest — city in the country. It became the poorest.

— Lyle Saxon,
   Fabulous New Orleans, 1928

STREET CRIES;
RECONSTRUCTION

Streetsell mammy, tignon tied
above black brow and wide,
    Ramineau! Ramineau!
no fees coming from agencies
to mammy-doll celebrities...
    Bel calas, bel tout-chauds!
show me how.

    Now if you want to dribe 'way sorrow,
    Come an hear dis song tomorrow.
Look away, look away, look away, Dixieland.

    Bel calas, calas tout-chauds,
    In yo mouf an down dey go.
Look away.
    Hot rice fritters, sof' as snow,
    Bel calas, calas tout-chauds.
Look away.
Look away.
    VeeeejaTEBbles, got em fresh an sweet.
Sweat-certain, cotton-clad, cotton-haired,
pressed flesh against stucco gone brick,
    Ahm down in de street wid
    VeeeejaTEBbles!
red and white on black on white on red,
pleading up at iron-vined windows.
    Black-BAAAY-ry!

Sugar in de gourd an stony batter,
Whites grow fat an de niggers fatter.
Look away, look away, look away, Dixieland.

Free at last to look away, to beg
    Black-baay-ry, black-baay-ry!
the kind, kind, kindness of prices paid
    Fresh fum de vine, berry fine.
not for your children, for what your pot
holds, for whatever you've got
    Brroooooom man's comIN
    Shine?
in your basket, your shawl, on your head,
in your apron, your stall, on your bed.
    Ramineau!
Black jew woman, landless,
wandring drummer,
    Black-baay-ry!
summer pent, rented down,
    Straaaawbry, sweet to eat.
womb-curst mother to my mother too,
    Calas chauds, chauds, chauds!
wonder when you knew, you knew
    VejaTEBbles!
you'd sold old Dixie to your daughters.
    Ooooooh, shine!

Praline mammy, tignon tied,
cotton-headed, hope inside,
    Sweep out de chimbley, sweep out de heart'!
kids running up to kid you-all,
collecting no residual,

Ramineau! Hyeah come mah cart!
Started slow.

Hoe it down an scratch yo grabble,
To Dixie's land ah'm boun to trabble.
Look away, look away, look away, Dixieland.

Fat an roun, sugar sweet,
White an brown as girls you meet,
Pralines! Yes ma'am, pralines!
Yes ma'am!
Broad flat feet hobbling cobblestones
in your cast-off-slipper slow-drag rag
Rag an bone! Comin home!
Yes ma'am.
Ramineau, no, no, ramineau!
Slap the feet, feel the beat.
Oh, shine!
Sell the street by and buy,
Calas!
colored woman, black bury woman,
Herry, buy now, praline!
Praline! Sweep yo heart'!
Vejatebble, got sebble kine.
Broom man, sweep it clean!
Look away...
Berry fine calas, tout, tout-chauds!
Po-po-po-po, clo'spole,
lady?
Look away...

53

The community recognized the supreme domination of the "gentleman" in questions of right and of "the ladies" in matters of sentiment. Under such conditions, strength establishes over weakness a showy protection which is the sub-tlest of tyrannies, yet which ...constitutes (a woman) an autocrat of public sentiment and thus accepts her narrowest prejudices and most belated errors as the very need-be's of social life...In those days Creole society was a ship, in which the fair sex were all passengers and the ruder sex the crew.

— George Washington Cable,
The Grandissimes, 1880

THE STORYVILLE STORY

Monique de la Monde is the little-known heroine who became the first professional woman in the colonies. There are no statues to her memory. No one lights candles for her soul at the Church of the Immaculate Conception on Baronne Street. Even her grave is unmarked. But Monique laid the way.

It was never her intention to come to the colony. She was taking a consumer poll in Plesy when a local constable mistook her for a cutpurse. Monique assumed she was being loaded on a wagon for the provincial workhouse, but she found herself shackled in the hold of a sometime slaver, rocking in the harbor at L'Orient. It was only by virtue (so to speak) of the second mate's attentiveness that she was able to endure the five-month passage.

The second mate, whose name is lost to history, left the ship near what is now Galliano and sped via stolen horse upriver to New Orleans. Appropriately disguised, he met Monique at dockside and led her to a room above a tavern, *le Roi d'Exile*. She had to push past an advance line of gentlemen callers to make her way up the stairs.

Thus, in New Orleans, the oldest profession truly was, at least for women. Male prostitiution is not known to have arrived until much later.

Perhaps because the city quickly learned to tolerate the custom of mistress-keeping among the aristocracy, there was little indignation over more temporary programs of sexual release. The consumer-driven trade prospered.

Into the port poured trappers and traders, sailors and soldiers, teamsters and travelers — all of them men and most of them ready to part with their money at the slightest provocation. The provocation was provided by the Company of the Indies at first, but before long ladies of the evening were working their way downriver on keelboats. Just as the nutria thrived in Louisiana marshes after it was imported from South America, so did these immigrant night flowers take root and blossom here. Work was steady.

It was the aftermath of the War Between the States, Reconstruction, that broke the back of local tolerance. Before the War, the city's Common Council had been content merely to bar "notoriously abandoned" women from keeping shop on the street-floors of buildings. In its Ordinance No. 3267 of 1857, the Council cut itself in on the take by selling licenses. Prostitutes were to pay $100 a year, madames $250. Their research suggested the city could clear up to $100,000 a year in license fees alone. That would be about 69 madames and 827 prostitutes licensed.

But that ordinance was ruled unconstitutional and before long the again-unregulated prostitutes were thicker than filé gumbo. With Americanization of the city, even the old, unwritten codes of acceptable behavior were crumbling. Steamshipping crowded the riverside districts with seamen, dockhands, gamblers, and rough customers. Wives of politicians suffered verbal abuse from streetwalkers as they traveled to and from the opera.

Something had to be done.

It was January 1887 when Alderman Sidney Story took matters into his own hands. Story was a solid citizen of New Orleans' American Sector — everything on the upriver side of Canal Street. He was also a traveler who had passed a pleasurable moment or two within the red light districts of certain European cities. Story decided to get the local girls off the street and into the whorehouses where they belonged. Put all the whorehouses together and certain people would know where not to go. Others would enjoy the convenience.

Story's ordinance permitting prostitution (though not actually *legalizing* it) became law in July 1887. As Bienville was the first to illustrate, in Louisiana the truth bends as readily as the river. Buried in the middle of the legislation is the phrase, "… provided that nothing herein shall be so construed as to authorize any lewd woman to occupy a house, room or closet in any portion of the city." In other words, no matter what you read in this law, prostitution is still against the law.

What Story's ordinance artfully accomplished was to set boundaries, outside of which the law would be *enforced*. But within the district, the law would look the other way. Everybody understood this; no one in the city slept through passage of Story's legislation. Eventually two separate bordello districts were established, one in the French Sector, the other in the American Sector. The first ran from what is now Iberville Street to St. Louis Street, between North Basin and North Robertson; on the American side of Canal, the district ran from Franklin to Locust, between Gravier and Perdido. Together the two sections comprised about forty square blocks, collectively dubbed in honor of the man who cleaned up the town: Storyville.

Those square blocks filled up fast. Just a couple of years into the twentieth century, New Orleans could boast more than 2,000 whores, an increase of 142 percent in just fifty years. There were 230 sporting houses in Storyville, plus 30 "houses of assignation." The wine and food vendors, the furniture and piano dealers, the interior decorators and the cops on the beat all got their shares of the action. Storyville, even had its own yellow-page directory, although it was called The Blue Book, from the color of the ink on its cover.

In its preface the editors stated: "Everybody who knows to-day from yesterday will say that the Blue Book is the right book for the right people." The book contained "nothing but the facts" and was said to be "of the greatest value to strangers." Each girl was listed "alphabetically, under the headings 'white' and 'colored,' from alpha to omega. The names in capitals are landladies only."

The natural tendency for a modern scholar coming upon a copy of the directory is to quickly scan it for possible ancestors. No doubt more would be found if the Blue Book listed frequent customers along with the ladies. There are no fewer than twenty "Smiths" listed in one edition, just three of whom were "Colored." Also under the letter "S" can be found the Simms sisters — Bertha, Bella, Frances, and Stella — who worked together at 1565 Conti.

In the back of the book were ads for the better establishments, including photos of the parlors and boudoirs, plus some artfully worded descriptions.

For Gypsy Shaffer's at Iberville and North Villere:

In going the rounds, don't forget to meet Gipsy, and especially her array of feminine beauties. They are all clever. The head of the house, 'Gipsie,' will let nothing pass toward making life a pleasure.

For The Club at 327 N. Franklin:

Pretty Miss Maud Hartman, who has the high position as President of the Club, is one of those jolly fellows who has the support of all those who have joined the Club....The Club is one of the few gorgeously furnished places in Storyville and is located so that the most particular person can reach it without being seen.

For Willie Piazza's at 315 N. Basin:

The Countess Piazza has made it a study to try and make everyone jovial who visits her house. If you have the 'blues,' the Countess and her girls can cure them. She has, without doubt, the most handsome and intelligent octoroons in the United States. You should see them; they are all entertainers.

At Jessie Brown's there was "an array of beautiful women who know how to entertain properly and cleverly the most fastidious gentleman." Annie Ross, mistress of the Star Mansion, was "the Queen of Smile." Jessie Orloff was the "idol of society and club boys." At Marguerite and Diana's "everything goes as it will, and those that cannot be satisfied there must surely be of a queer nature. They are also known for their singing and dancing." On the other hand, Grace Lloyd, a "woman of very rare attainments" and of "good old English stock," was reknowned for the "grand and rare collection of Art Tapestry" at her North Franklin Street palace.

Those were some of the famous places. There were lots of other spots written up in the histories and novels and letters home. Lulu White's, Tom Anderson's Cafe, the Haymarket, Josie Arlington's. They were the *society* houses, where it was just fine to be seen. The other type of establishment was ably described by the late jazz drummer, Paul Barbarin, interviewed by Clint Bolton in the April 1973 *New Orleans Magazine.*

Barbarin grew up drumming in Storyville during its last years, 1915 to 1917. He played the spots of lesser reknown, like the Tuxedo Club and The 25 Club. "I remember the dice-shooters, the sportin' women and the sports." He recalls "notorious women" like Mary Meathouse and Mary Jack-the-Bear, "real mean women. Gal named Lily Crips, cause she walked kinda gimpy. She was a little dark woman, always in jail. Mighty tough."

And on Monday nights at The 25 Club, Barbarin recalled fondly the "ham kicks" that would draw the customers on an otherwise slow night, the way bars use Monday Night Football nowadays.

"Man, that was wild. They's take this ham on a string and hang it up real high. The gal that kicked the highest and showed the most, she got the ham."

You can just hear Barbarin's drum rolls and cymbal crashes.

Which brings up a point about jazz. Was Storyville really its "cradle"?

Music was a part of every evening's entertainment at a Storyville bordello. Consequently, every parlor needed a piano. Now, there were three types of pianists in New Orleans in those days. There were Sunday afternoon amateur recitalists, there were accompanists for the opera and church soloists, and there were boys who'd learned their music on the streets. Only the last were likely to apply for Storyville performances.

The music of the street and honkytonks had evolved considerably since the days of the dance in *Place Congo*, but the Afro-Caribbean rhythms were still there. The Creole

61

music had absorbed and mutated everything it touched, from brass-band marches to grand opera arias. Most of its practitioners were black. When they congregated in the street to play for nickels, they were known as "spasm bands."

Whites and blacks would gather on street corners to hear a spasm band "jass it up," until a man in blue arrived to disperse the crowds. "Jass," they say, was a black verb with sexual connotations, as in, "Jass me, baby." I have the relentless image of some New York journalist pontificating about the primitive "jass music" he encountered while doing purely journalistic research on the pleasure pits of Storyville. This account, in turn, would have been editorialized upon (with either indignation or sly disdain) by a New Orleans newspaper writer, whose typesetter mistook "ss" for "zz." This is my own, purely speculative, account of the origin of "jazz."

The jazzmen played, as Paul Barbarin told the story, for a dollar a night, so low was their estate. Fees at the sporting houses for girls were $25 the half-hour, $100 the evening. A five-dollar gold piece was the customary tip. Younger girls, offered as virgins, went for around three hundred, and there were fixed rates for every abberation, from pederasty to flagellation. The girls could at least take pride in being well paid; musicians swallowed pride and digested applause.

Then, just as jazz was starting to catch on in other parts of the country, Storyville went out of business. World War I was in full swing and the Secretary of the Navy did not like the idea of his sailors having such easy access to hooch and hookers as they had in New Orleans. The Navy flexed its muscle and prostitution went back underground, after twenty years of permitted illegality, in 1917.

The folk music of New Orleans, having finally found an

audience, was abandoned in the city of its birth. The musicians took their talent and their horns and their banjos and their drums and went up river. They went to St. Louis, to Kansas City, to Chicago, and New York. Whether or not New Orleans jazz actually began in Storyville — or in Congo Square — the history of jazz in New Orleans ends with the shutting down of Storyville. As Paul Barbarin said, "Them was scuffle days" for musicians in New Orleans. They still is.

ELBOW GREASE

Sly, sly, slide it in,
Slide it, sliiiiide it out.
Lemme hear ya mow, owe, own,
Lemme hear ya shout.
Pucker up some gravel, now.
Grate, great, grit and groan.
Easy rider, play it tighter.
Ride it, ride it,
Sly, aye, eyed it,
Sly......trombone.

"My-de'-seh," exclaimed M. Grandissime, suddenly becoming very earnest, "I am nothing, nothing! There-h is wheh you have the advantage of me. I am but a dilettante, whether-h in politics, in philosophy, morals, aw religion. I am afraid to go deeply into anything, lest it should make rhuin in my name, my family, my prhope'ty."

— George Washington Cable,
  The Grandissimes, 1880

"When I took the oath as Governor, I didn't take any vows of poverty."

— *Richard W. "Dick" Leche,*
Governor of Louisiana 1936-1939

A BRIEF HISTORY OF POLITICS
IN THE COLONY

My grandmother, who wore gloves and veiled hats to barbecues, would not permit the discussion of politics, particularly local politics, at the dinner table.

She had her reasons.

Now, I have known good, honest people in New Orleans who have carried their good intentions into Louisiana's political sludge. Rarely have I seen them crawl out again. They all believed they could change the system. Instead, the system changed them.

Patronage, influence peddling, vote buying, and pork barreling arrived here with the first colonial government. It prospered as duckweek prospers in Bayou Bienvenue.

For 250 years New Orleans has refused to look the other way. No-indeed-not (as my grandmother used to say.) We have kept our eyes glued to the game. We have cheered on the every play of our favorites. Our political arena is better than the Circus Maximus ever was, because here the emperors and senators are down there thrusting in the dust with all the other gladiators. It's a grand spectacle, as long as you're wrapped up in it.

When I grew up in Louisiana there was only one political party, and they called themselves Democrats. Republicans were two-headed sons of carpetbaggers. They were the party that put niggers in the state house during Reconstruction. We were still fighting that war a hundred years later. A black man couldn't drink from certain water fountains in City Hall, but if he passed the literacy test, he could vote for a Democratic candidate.

68

The big hero still (as he was forty years ago) is Huey Pierce Long. The Kingfish was ready to become the first Socialist dictator of the United States when they gunned him down. After his chosen successor, Dick Leche, ran the state just about into the ground, Huey's brother, "Uncle Earl" Long, took up residence in the governor's mansion. But Earl went crazy and ran off with a Bourbon Street stripper.

I could tell you lots of stories just as uplifting.

I could tell you about the good ol' senator who was the butt of every legislative party, where they sang songs about the senator's grocery store where he short-weighted meat and punched holes in domestic swiss so it'd look imported. I could tell you about the mayor who said we shouldn't believe any rumor unless it came from him, who said he would get the ball off on the right foot, who warned non-conformists away from New Orleans and who accused us of sitting on some of the greatest assets in the world. I could tell you about the sheriff who set up road blocks to keep black people out of his parish. I could tell you how they threw chicken wings and drumsticks across the lower house of the State Legislature one day and got mad when it made the news.

I could tell you stories, make you laugh till you'd cry. Lot of laughs in politics here. But, as my grandmother realized, none of those tales would make the food taste any better.

YOU PROBLY AIN'T
FUM LOOZYANA

Way down south where the sunbelt sags
Und'neath the Midwes' belly,
We buil' dem house on hemorrhoids
Sunk deep in petrolyum jelly.

We pray on Saddy evenin,
Go ballin Saddy night,
Sleep late on Sundy mawnin
Till the teevee football's right.

We'd stake our lives on our soul's redemption
An' Mardigraw balls an' the Homestead Exemption.
An' if that's too much for yo comprehension
Then you prob'ly think a plantain's
   just a ripe banana.
You prob'ly ain't
   fum Loozyana.

Mis'sippi River hauls America's sludge
Like a Stuckey's ovuhstocked wit divinity fudge,
But it's Loozyana plants pump the chemical waste
That gives the drinkin water its down-home taste.

We got boudin on our biscuits,
Red beans all ovuh our rice,
Oysters in our turkeys,
Dixie beer on ice.

We got lots goin on the News don't mention
Where they buy up yo vote wit a lifetime pension.
An' if it's all beyond yo comprehension,
Then you prob'ly think a plantain's
 just a ripe banana.
You probly ain't
 fum Loozyana.

We got gator, duck an' crawfish
Thick as turtle sauce-piquant.
We got evvy kind o' fishin
That a man could evuh want.

We got the Corps o' Engineers to drain
Our swamps an' ebb our flow
For plantin soybeans Uncle Sam
Gon' pay us not to grow.

We used to have dem pirates
Till the well-heads come aroun'
An' we start payin plenny
For dat gas down in our groun'...

Is it still outside yo comprehension?
Well, we t'ank you kin'ly f' y'all's attention,
But you mus' be stuck in another die-mension,
You won't never tell a plantain
 fum a ripe banana.

You sure as hell ain't
 fum Loozyana.

Not without its amusing feature was the violent Creole objection to the Act of the Legislature of 1899 creating the (New Orleans) Sewerage and Water Board. A sewerage system was to be installed, and also a water purification plant. The Creoles suspected trickery. Sanitary toilets were to be used, and they were going to make you buy water to flush them! To save the measure and appease the Creoles, the law was actually amended to provide free water for flushing toilets in New Orleans.

— *John Churchill Chase,*
  Frenchmen, Desire, Good Children and
  Other Streets of New Orleans, 1949

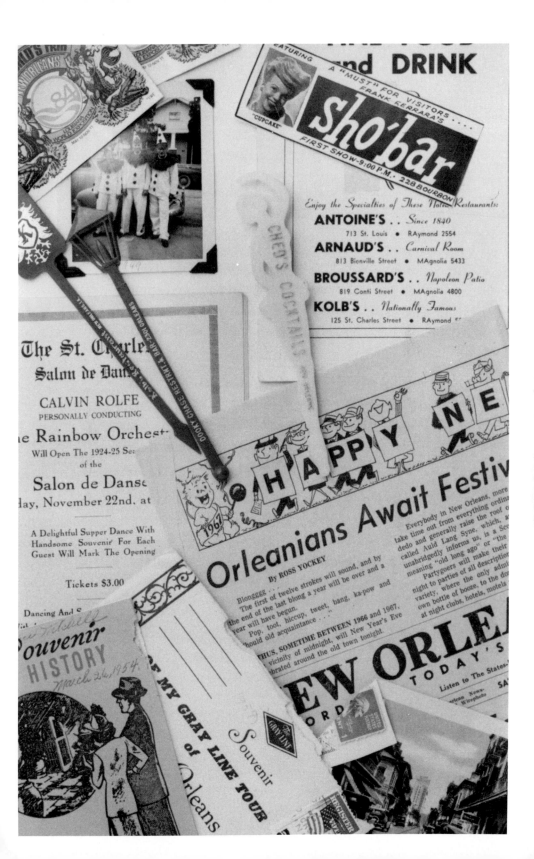

He would never tire of it...Mardi Gras was threaded through the warp and woof of their very lives: it was tradition; it was their strongest link with youth; they worshipped it as the symbol of all joie de vivre . Although for the rest of the year they made believe they were blasé, and said that they wished Mardi Gras could be done away with...still, when Mardi Gras came around again, these same old gentlemen would make any sacrifice to "go out," as they called it: would get up out of a sick bed and risk pneumonia during a cold snap, to shiver in pink tights, teeth chattering, high up on a float that joggled for hours through the streets.

— *Edward LaRoque Tinker,*
Mardi Gras Masks, 1931

A DIET OF FAT TUESDAYS

Is it any wonder, I wonder, we're all so worldly here? At least once a year, often more often, we cut ourselves new out of whole cloth. As the song of the Mardi Gras Indians puts it:

"Every year, at Connival time, I make a new suit."

Not just a few of us, not just Rex and Comus and the Queen of Nefertiri and Zulu. Everybody does it, or so close to everybody that it's the leftovers who feel left out. It's all a bit like the Mad Hatter's tea party. Clean cup, clean cup. Move down. Pick a persona, climb into a costume. Be a Barbary ape or Barbara Fritchie. Or wear the ultimate disguise: go naked. Now we have plastic covers for your body parts so you can look naked and not be. Identity is never a crisis at the Mardi Gras.

My young life is a succession of costumes. I was a big blue bird with orange feet. I was a little prince. A clown, a gypsy, a Chinaman, a Mexican, a sheep in wolf's clothing with my Red Ridinghood. I was an enormous hat. I was a pink elephant, a sphinx in red flannel underwear. All this imagination, energy, and craft to be other than myself. Every year at Carnival time I make a new suit.

What we think we're doing, I think, is making up new selves, leaving the old ones like crabs leave their old shells. There's that moment of magic, Mardi Gras morning, when we rush about the house, pulling bits and pieces together at the last minute or carrying out long-simmering conspiracies. Men putting on makeup. Children growing fangs. I leave the house a New Man. I am Reborn.

T'row me sump'n mistah!

A diet of Fat Tuesdays may do irreparable harm. It may

leave us believing it really is that easy to slip from one lie into another, that harmless. It may leave us supposing we can walk out the church on Sunday and come back for ashes on Wednesday without paying for all the loudmouthed, inconsiderat, ass-pinching, shoving, swilling, rude debauchery we've wrought in the meantime. A life of Fat Tuesdays makes one weak, to paraphrase the old schoolkid joke.

Easter is supposed to be the Resurrection, Ash Wednesday the death-symbol. The tale told of Mardi Gras is that it is our final day to enjoy the pleasures we must forsake for the forty days to come. But we've turned it all around here. Mardi Gras is the season (no longer just a day) when we may exhibit publicly the gross behavior our families and friends must endure in private the rest of the year. Lent is the season of eating crawfish instead of meat, because crawfish are more fun and so plentiful then as to be cheap. Easter is when the Mardi Gras clubs begin regrouping for next Mardi Gras. Easter we start making our new suits. It is the beginning of Advent.

Damn but it's fun though, Mardigraw day, jumpin' up from them curbstones and ladders and pushin' aside the people around you (except when you realize it was an old lady or a little kid and then you have to give 'em what you got to make 'em feel better and to make you feel better too) and you feel your hand tighten around a pair o'beads and the little plastic balls slide away between your fingers or it's a doubloon that you never can catch especially at night and it bounces and you hear it pop the bald dome of the guy in front and then ping down on the pavement and you have to go down for it in the footsmashin' heelcrushin' gutter and hope you miss the spot where sheriff Harry Lee's fat white horse laid a turd.

Damn but it's fun.

EARLY IN THE MORNING

Early in the morning on the Avenue,
Didn't see me but I saw you.
Saw some fools in muddy spats,
Bobbing canes and bowler hats,
Cruising through the crowds for hours
Paying for kisses with paper flowers.
Saw African Indians waving flags,
Zulu cowboys on swaybacked nags.
Saw whites playing blacks playing whites,
*   painted black.*
Saw people catching trinkets throwing them
*   back.*
Saw plastic bottoms through arm-high slits.
Saw pinwheels whirling on plastic tits.
Saw kids who'd kill for a bamboo spear,
Showing no mercy, showing no fear.
Saw tooth-gone crones in widows' weeds
Prone under ladders for worthless beads.
Drank a few brews, broke a few necks,
Got me a place in time for Rex.
Mardi Gras morning on the Avenue,
Didn't see me but I saw you.

succession of costumes

ZULU

in time f...
Rex

CITY OF NEW ORLEANS
DELESSEPS S. MORRISON, MAYOR
CARNIVAL 1957
PROTEUS PARADE
MONDAY NIGHT, MARCH 4
TICKET - - - - - - - - - - - - - - - $1.20
The City of New Orleans is not responsible for Cancellation of Parades. No refund will be made for this ticket.

SECTION B
LEE CIRCLE STANDS

They call 'em gays, we call 'em Belmonters. What a mess? Can one imagine human beings defying the Holy Redeemer and the natural laws of male and female. Man wuz made to mate with the female and match up their instruments...If they all want to go to Cat Island and play Who's Got the Button or something, let them be, but keep them away from our children....When they get ready for the River Styx and look down at their creative organs that should have helped propogate the race and say all that we're looking at are dead entries. They can also holler above to their parents and say, "If youse wuz like us, we wouldn't be here."

—Prieur Leary,
Tower of Babblers, 1983

Show me any Creole, or any number of Creoles, in any sort of contest, and right down at the foundation of it all, I will find you this same preposterous, apathetic, fantastic, suicidal pride. It is as lethargic and ferocious as an alligator. That is why the Creole always is (or thinks he is) on the defensive.

— *George Washington Cable,*
  The Grandissimes, 1880

DOIN' THE CARNIVAL DRAG

"Where do I go to get a ringside seat for the *He-Sheba Contest?*"

The large, lumpy man at the grill turned his hamburger and pressed it hard with a long-handled spatula. He looked over his shoulder, hairy and bare except for the undershirt strap, and considered his answer. At last he said, "Ain't never hoid o' nuttin' bah dat name."

He slapped a tinfoil plate on the burger and weighted it down with an old St. Joseph brick. To one side of his grill he had a stack of plates and a stack of bricks. I had never seen hamburgers pressed this way. "You talkin' about de *Bourbon Street Awards*, maybe?"

I understood. The event was called one thing by us outsiders, another by those in the know. He resented the implications of "He-Sheba." He probably was not gay. His two other customers, sharing a *Times-Picayune* over coffee at the far end of the counter, probably were.

"We had de BBC film it lashyeah," he said. He smeared his hands across the front of an apron that was wider than it was long and browner than it was white. "Dose mudduhfuckuhs at City Hall ack like dey nevuh hoid o' us."

It was not difficult to separate myself from such wrongheaded detractors. In the end, the fat man's information was better than his hamburger, but I only had to pay for the hamburger.

The nation's largest annual gathering of transvestites had begun, he said, as his own idea, back in 1960. The following year, on Mardi Gras day, the first costume contest was held in the 900 block of Bourbon Street. He organized it and had a platform built so the contestants could be seen above the crowds. He rented a public address system so the announcer could be heard above the din. All this to help beer and burger sales during the carnival season. But in recent years he had grown more and more irritated by the "mudduhfuckuhs" at City Hall. What with permits, licenses, police for crowd control, political palm-greasing, and admonitions from the Fire Marshall, it hardly seemed worth it.

That's when the boys from *Lafitte's In Exile* stepped in. The costume contest had grown dear to their hearts and they were not going to let it gurgle down the drain of bureaucratic apathy. This year, the fat man told me, the contest was all their show. And they could damn well have it.

Lafitte's In Exile is a marvelous dive. Just down the street from *Lafitte's Blacksmith Shop*, where the great pirate, cut-throat, thief, probable rapist, and local hero is said to have planned some of his exploits. There is no sign outside *Lafitte's In Exile* that proclaims it as a "gay bar." Nevertheless, I could not help feeling like an Eskimo in Afghanistan when I walked in.

The bartender was...let's call him "Jamey."

"You want to write about the co-*o-on* test! That is so *sweet*. I can't wait for next week. Oh, yes, honey, I'll be there with balls on — I mean *bells*. Silly me."

Jamey told me how the contest would be judged — Best Child's Costume, Best Group Costume, Best Drag Costume, and Best All-Around Costume. "'Course they generally *have* to give that one to the drag queen winner. They're the ones who go really all out. So they deserve it, y'know?"

Jamey told me the contest would be held right outside *Lafitte's* and that I could buy a ticket for a seat on the balcony of the bar for just ten dollars. He told me he's never heard of the "He-Sheba" name and said it was probably made up by that "gross old man who runs the tacky diner. Isn't he Middle Eastern or something?"

I asked Jamey about the big attraction of putting on gaudy female costumes.

"Oh, well, you know," he began, leaning over with both elbows on the bar and his chin resting on intertwined fingers, "it's kind of a chance to express another side of yourself. *You* know."

Jamie is a little too short, a little too round, a little too soft to make a convincing man. He has a young woman's face with big, expressive eyes. His nails are longer than most men's and well manicured at the ends of supple fingers. His every sentence contains italics.

"Some people say everybody's got two sides, you know? Well, I know *I* do. *All* of *us* do. All year long we have to go around like *this?*" He straightened up and did a half turn to show me his outfit: blue oxford shirt with rolled-up sleeves and navy slacks, brown penny loafers without socks. "Well, this is our big *chance*, you know? I mean, this is the *only* day of the whole year we get to show off our other half. And, if you ask me, it's the *better* half. Aside from that it's just a whole lot of *fu-u-un*. With the competition, a *lot* of 'em really go berserk. I mean, too *much*. *I* just want to see if I can look prettier and more feminine than the other guys."

I paid my ten dollars to a man upstairs. My name went on a list and that was my only receipt. As I left, Jamey blew me a kiss — his idea of a joke, knowing I was "straight" — and called, "Now I'm gonna *look* for you next Tuesday and tell you 'Hi' if you don't recognize me."

Now I couldn't wait for Mardi Gras either.

This was 1973 and a lot of things have changed since then. A lot of closet doors have opened. Things may be better now for the French Quarter homosexual crowd, but at that Mardi Gras you wouldn't have found many to say things could *get* any better.

"Wouldja look at the size o' *that* stud!"

Muriel, sitting next to me on the narrow balcony, was pointing to an Adonis, complete with laurel wreath, in the street below. Instead of a toga he wore the tightest-fitting jeans I'd ever seen, girls' jeans. His all-too-public parts were sculpted in blue denim. "Wadd'ya suppose *he's* sellin'?"

Overweight and fifty-ish, dressed in a cowgirl outfit, Muriel smoked brown cigarettes and drank Old Crow. One or both of those was generally in the left hand, used for punctuation and broad gestures. Muriel was what they called a "fag hag." She got her kicks hanging around with gay men. She lived in the central part of the state but never failed to make it to New Orleans for the Mardi Gras.

"There's Freddie," she hollered. I felt a splash of Old Crow in my lap as she leaned over the rickety wrought-iron railing. "Fred-DEE! Fred-DEE!" Her voice boomed but the curly-haired blond boy across the street did not take notice. He was dressed all in leather, cap to boots, and he had four male companions in identical outfits.

"Ain't he a dish?" Muriel enquired. "I met him at Corinne Dunbar's the other night. He was there with my old pal, George. Now George don't know *I* know, you know? I mean he don't know I know he's gay. Weee-yull, sweetie, when I saw *that* I had to just stand up in the middle o' that restaurant and holler. I said, 'George, I just *love* your new boyfriend there. If he goes an' gets tired o' you, now, you be sure to send him over to Muriel, ya hear? Muriel'll take

85

care o'*you*, honey.' Weee-yull, everybody in that there restaurant musta turned around an' stared. They was some embarrassed. But it don't matter none 'cause we're all good friends. I tell you what, I believe it was the most fun I ever *did* have. You shoulda seen the look on that beautiful face."

"Freee-deee," she called out, "up here."

Leather Fred at last turned his limpid gaze on our balcony and the recognition registered in his face. He said something to his companions and they formed a line, facing us, smiling and waving. At Freddie's signal, they turned together and stuck their rumps in the air, pointing in our direction. The bottoms were cut out from their leather pants. Each member of the chorus line grabbed a cheek of the one beside him and pinched. We could hear their squeals in our perch.

Muriel roared, stomped her feet, spilled her drink, and nearly put out her brown cigarette on my nose.

Jamey came out on the balcony in time to catch the tail end of the show and grimaced. "Oh, puh-*leez*," he said. "If that isn't the tackiest thing I ever saw I'll eat my brassiere."

Jamey was a living doll. He sported a strawberry blonde wig and a flowing pink-and-lavender Gucci caftan, his roundness elaborated upon in the appropriate places. I told him hello and he said, "Oh, *poo*, you recognized me."

He took Muriel's empty glass and turned to fetch a refill, but his spiked heel caught in a crack of the wooden balcony and he tumbled into Muriel's lap, a situation she could not ignore, especially with her drink hand free. When Jamey slapped Muriel's hand and rose to go, she told him he had no business wearing high heels if he couldn't walk in them.

"You just don't worry about *me*, sweetheart, 'cause I'm a lot more comfortable in heels than you are and they do a whole lot more *damage* than flats, if you know what I mean."

The street around the wooden platform filled and Stan the Clown, night bartender at *Lafitte's*, took up the microphone to emcee. Because of the way the loudspeakers were positioned, we on the balcony could not hear very well. But we had an unimpeded view of the action.

I can't recall seeing any children's costumes from that balcony. Freddie and the leather boys did their turn on the stage. A family of butterflies showed up. There were several pairs which, I was told, qualified as "groups." Most memorable of these was the Great White Hunter with his chained gorilla. The chest of the gorilla suit was carefully cut away to reveal what seemed to be a large set of human female breasts. A sign on the ape's back read: "Only Topless Gorilla in Captivity."

A balcony on Bourbon Street Mardi Gras day is not a place for the squeamish. There was a man in a "Colonel Sanders" costume who continually licked his middle finger ("Finger-lickin' good," remember?) and waved it like a scepter to the crowd. Another man came up wearing a woman's girdle and home-made pasties, with tassels; he was fat and quite ugly. There was also a giant roll of toilet paper. We watched in wonder as a tall, thin man worked his way through literally wall-to-wall crowds, wearing a peacock costume. His remarkable feathered tail stretched almost from curb to curb. He had to mount the platform sideways and when he bowed, the tail feathers stretched clear over his head and nearly pushed Stan the Clown over the platform railing. The crowd applauded in admiration.

Of course, it was a drunken crowd and not hard to please. They went crazy over an "Indian" in elaborate headress, wearing nothing else but smeared warpaint and a blood-stained bandage wrapped around his dangling apparatus. When I inquired as to the significance of the bandage, Muriel replied, "Well, sugar, you heard o' wounded knee...."

There were transvestites in seemingly inexhaustible supply. I do not understand, nor do I need to find out, how it is some men grow breasts and seem to lose their appendages. All I can tell you is that there were a lot more of the former than the latter and yet, and yet, these creatures were all of them male. I took pictures that day and sometimes get them out, just to marvel. Often you can identify the men by their faces, and nearly always from their hands. But you have to look close. Women are just as amazed as the men in the slide show audience to learn that the cleavage and crotches are not female.

As the show wore on, we were joined on the balcony by a stylishly dressed gentleman in an Austin-Reed jacket and sharply creased trousers. His only concession to the spirit of the day was a large sequined mask that covered nearly his entire face. Muriel greeted his entrance with a display of affection, finding a way to plant a wet kiss on the small part of his face that was exposed. He was introduced as "Mister Domino," Muriel bragging that she knew his real name. He was there to see without being seen and he came equipped with opera glasses. As he took a seat, he also produced from his pocket a yard-long strand of silver-and-gold beads and draped them around his neck.

"Honey-bun, those are simply breath-taking," Muriel exclaimed. "Wherever did you get them?"

"They were last year's favor at Prometheus," said Mr. Domino. His voice was rich, with something in it like a trace of the Islands. He spoke softly, but the voice cut through or floated above the racket from the street below. "I wore them to the Carrollton Parade on Sunday and some vicious son of a bitch tried to pull them off my neck. They broke, but I managed to salvage most of the beads. I spent all Sunday night restringing them. I don't know why Carnival has to bring out the beast in some people. Do you really like them?"

"Stunning," Muriel replied. "And how was the ball? Nobody invited *me* this year."

Domino ignored the implication of rudeness. "It was truly marvelous. The theme was the Thirteen Signs of the Zodiac and the costumes were magnificent. Exquisite. The Taurus was my favorite, horns out to *here*. And the Gemini twins...You would have died right there in the Longshoreman's Hall, Muriel."

The old-line "respectable" balls are always held in Municipal Auditorium. But in the weeks leading up to Mardi Gras, the auditorium, an old barn where Congo Square used to be, is all booked up. The newcomers have to take what they can get. There is a nice irony about the gay balls being held at the I.L.A. hall, where brothers of brawn and boister stand each morning to begin their manly labors.

I asked Domino whether his organization was the only carnival association of its kind. "Good heavens, no," he answered. "Nor the eldest. Simply the best. Those animals in Yuga started it all."

"Damned near finished it, too," Muriel broke in, laughing.

"Quite right. The imbeciles went across the river and put on their ball in Plaquemines Parish. Can you believe it? We are talking about the last bastion of the Ku Klux Klan. Those are dangerous people over there. Well, naturally they got themselves all drunk and rowdy."

"Boys will be boys, boys." Muriel adored her own humor.

"They all thought: Well, here we are at the end of the

goddam *world*. Nobody's going to give a good goddam *what* we do. And so, of course, they're all naked and into this and into that when the police run in with their big dogs and their big sticks. They tell me Leander Perez himself was there to lead the righteous assault. The Judge."

"I mean to tell you," Muriel squawked, "there was skin flyin' in every direction! An awful lot o'people took to the swamps *that* night, honey."

"And since our faithful and true friends at *The* good old *Times-Picayune* faithfully and truthfully printed the name of every person arrested, a good many nice people lost a good many fine jobs. Ever since that night we have become more licensed and less licentious, if you follow my meaning. Of course, after the ball is over...." Mr. Domino hummed in his gentle baritone.

At that moment there was a commotion down the street that threatened to overpower the commotion below. Muriel leaned over the railing, dropping her lady's cigar, to better inform us on the disturbance. "I'll be a dirty son of a bitch," she screamed. "Some certified asshole's trying to get a truck down here."

I leaned over the rail for a better view. Muriel was right. An 18-wheeler was pushing through the Bourbon Street crowds, slow but deadly. People were screaming. Stan the Clown was shouting at the driver through his P. A. system. But the driver kept coming, refusing to let up on the cord of his air horn. The red truck was like a wounded, enraged animal, coming on at whatever cost.

It was a truck that had been in a Mardi Gras parade, Elks or Crescent City, following the Rex Organization. Its maskers had disembarked, but you could make out a "little-Spanish-town" motif in the crepe paper and papier mache festooning the trailer. The driver could only have been drunk.

"There ain't nowhere for those people to go, you bastard!" Muriel was screaming at the driver, half a block away. "They're packed in there like anchovies. Jesus, somebody's gonna get themselves killed."

But the crowds in the street had long parted with their inhibitions and now Stan the Clown began urging them to violence. People in costumes were climbing onto the bumper and fenders of the truck. Others were clambering up the trailer, others tearing at the decorations. "Colonel Sanders" started helping other people aboard. Somehow somebody got a part of the truck's hood raised up.

All of a sudden there was "Wounded Knee," the near-naked Indian, riding the roof of the cab like it was a war pony. He was whooping and waving his arms in the air and he was holding what looked like the truck's carburetor wires. The beast was stopped dead in its tracks. The driver locked himself in and pulled for all he was worth on that air horn.

"Whooey, honey, that truck ain't goin' nowhere!" Muriel was overcome with joy. She gave me a bear hug and yet another Old Crow bit the dust, or in this case bit the back of my shirt. There was a siren in the distance and policemen on horseback edged their nervous mounts through the crowds. "Here comes the cavalry!" Muriel whooped.

She turned to share the good news with her well-dressed friend, but Mister Domino was gone. "Shit," she said, "that man's so nervous he won't even pee in a trough. You'd think them cops was comin' for the express purpose of findin' out who's that ol' fag on the balcony at Lafitte's In Exile."

Going to fetch herself another drink, she paused at the door and winked at me. "On second thought, honey, if they knew, you and me could be on the six o'clock news."

I read in the *Picayune* the next morning that a new record for Mardi Gras garbage had been established — more than fifteen hundred tons. I read that someone had been arrested for throwing live white mice from a float. I read a columnist's comments on "the prodigies of enthusiasm that can be generated by papier mache." And I read that Ash Wednesday was listed on Roman calendars as "*initium jejunii*" and not as "the Day After Mardi Gras." I read nothing about the truck overwhelmed by transvestites and a naked Indian.

"*Memento homo,*" the priest used to tell me, unaware that "homo" was the ultimate insult to a boy of my persuasion. "*Memento homo, quia pulvis es, et in pulverum revertis.*"

The pretzel was invented in honor not of beer but of Lent. It is unleavened. There's nothing but flour, water, and salt in an honest pretzel, and its tiny arms are folded across its chest in Lenten prayer.

Pretzels are good with beer, however, and beer is excellent with crawfish, and crawfish are what Lent is all about, I suspect.

THE CITY THAT CARE FORGOT

Way down yonder, down in old New Orleans,
Your heart grows fonder, ponderin Dixie's Darlins,
Setting on the stoop in the broad daylight,
Wrapped around the streetlamps late at night.

Welcome to the land of Creole cheese and pralines,
Milk and honey gone hard on those dreamy dreams.
You had to try her on and you love the fit,
Got the feel of all the sins you'd love to commit.

The City that Care Forgot,
she's got a new believer.
She's a deceiver, but your fever's up,
You'll never want to leave her again.

Her architecture's texture's got a pox so pretty
And when jazz jukes lecture in the mean Queen City
You get misty with the thrill of her history,
So you swill to the gills with her mystery.

Bars on all her windows, bars on all her blocks,
Pousse cafés and dubonnets, herbsainte on the rocks,
Ramos fizzes, hurricanes, sweet sazeracs.
Head on up to heaven on her streetcar tracks.

She's the City that Care Forgot,
you've got to possess her.
She'll be professor, your confessor too,
As soon as you undress her she's yours.

93

Head for family fun in her fab French Quarter.
Just walk behind your son (who's talking to your daughter?)
When you start seeing bulges where they shouldn't be
Then you'd best stop indulging in that fantasy.

Mules, hot, trotting down the streets of Sodom.
Dancers, hot and hip, stripping top and bottom.
Close enough to smell, the city bares her soul,
Mellow, swelling belly, sells her jelly roll

> *She's the City that Care Forgot*
> *and she's yours for the taking.*
> *She's just aching to be shaken up.*
> *Don't wake her, though, she's taking it slow.*

"Vie cannari ka fé bon bouillon."

"It's the old pot that makes the good soup."

— *Creole proverb*

Anyone who has ever paid a flying visit to New Orleans probably knows something about those various culinary preparations whose generic name is "gombo" — compounded of many odds and ends, with the okra plant, or true gombo for a basis, but also comprising occasionally "losé, zepinard, laitie," and other vegetables sold in bunches in the French Market.

— *Lafcadio Hearn,*
  Gombo Zhebes, 1885

ROUX THE DAY

In Italy they say a meal without wine is like a day without sunshine. In New Orleans we get by just fine without sunshine, but good food and drink are at least as essential as oxygen. Everybody here is a cook. By conservative estimate, a new Louisiana or New Orleans cookbook rolls off the presses every six weeks. The irony in this is that no Louisiana cook worth his or her garlic salt would ever follow a written recipe.

But you have to start somewhere. My wife will consult a cookbook now and then, skimming over a recipe just to get the general feel of it, then return the book to the shelf. At that point she's ready to tackle the ingredients in her own way. When a new ingredient comes along, she'll rummage around in her memories till she hits on something similar and then she'll approach the stove with confidence.

For example, there's a Japanese plum tree in our back yard. Probably one-third of the back yards in New Orleans have Japanese plum trees. Their yellow, ping-pong ball-sized fruit is fairly sour, like a kumquat. When we were kids we used to eat them to prove our courage. Mostly we would throw them at each other. I've heard them called several names but only rarely "loquat," which is what they are. Loquats hail not from Japan but from China. I don't know how they got here, but here they are.

Last April our loquat was loaded with ripe fruit. Our daughter, Lauren Beth, got the urge to pick some and before long she had a big Dorignac's grocery bag full. "Let's make some Japanese plum jam," I said.

97

"Okay," said Joann, "you peel the plums."

After what seemed like hours of peeling, washing, and popping out pits, we had just half a pot filled with juicy pulp. The payoff in fruit is small compared to the labor. "What now?" I asked.

"Just follow Grandma's recipe," my wife answered.

"But your grandmother never cooked these things."

"I don't know. She might have. And if she did she would have used about one cup of sugar to two cups of fruit. That looks like about four cups of fruit, so we'll add two cups of sugar and turn on the heat. Then we'll add a little lemon."

"Why lemon?"

"You always put some lemon in."

Words like "some," "a little," "about," "always," and "to taste" are among the most commonly used in a New Orleans cook's lexicon. We added some lemon, stirred "frequently" and turned off the fire when the stuff looked "ready." It was stupendous, a cross between orange marmalade and peach preserves. Put it on toast, croissants, or bagels and you'll never let another spring go by without raiding a loquat tree.

Our restaurants may be famous, but this is the kind of cooking that has made New Orleans what it is today — overweight and happy to be here. Among the very best at this free-style cooking was Joann's grandmother, Vivian Dudossat Allen. She was short and round and beautiful and everybody called her Grandma.

On a crisp fall day, when the big windows in the back room next to the kitchen were open, you could pull into the driveway and know Grandma was up to something good. It almost always started with a roux, and the aroma of a roux cooking down in an old black skillet is something you can't set down on paper.

Grandma made her roux with some chopped-up onions

and garlic, parsley, a bay leaf, a little salt and a little water, some flour and some fat. She cooked it down slowly in her big black skillet, careful not to burn it, until it was brown and smooth. This was how she started her red beans and her gumbo, her stuffed mirlitons and her tomato gravy. While the roux was being made, Grandma was usually tending to one or two other chores, like fixing a batter to fry something in or getting a vegetable ready.

Frying was the way a great many things got cooked, and nobody could fry like Grandma. No fancy baskets and thermometers, just that big iron skillet on a gas stove and one fork. Her specialty was the French Fry. Crisp on the outside, soft in the middle and golden as a summer squash blossom. Every thick sliver was perfect. Her potatos have never been equaled in my experience.

There wasn't anything Grandma couldn't cook or wasn't willing to try. Grandpa Ernest Allen (She called him "Patsy") would come home from a hunting or fishing trip with rabbits, and coots, or *poules d'eau*, with conchs, and eels. Grandma would almost always come up with a recipe to make it palatable. The one exception I can recall were *poules d'eau* — that's pronouned "pull-doo," literally "water chickens" but more often called "mud ducks." I don't think anything could improve a mud duck. Grandma occasionally flinched at a challenge, but there were few vegetables or animals she couldn't lick. Even things like snapping turtles Grandpa brought home from work, out supervising some new construction for the Public Service. "Aw, Patsy," she'd say, "what I'm gonna do with that." She'd find something to do with it. If all else failed, there'd be snapping turtle gumbo.

Just as she never knew *what* to expect for supper, Grandma could never be sure *how many* she'd have to serve. Grandpa would bring a friend or two home. Her son and son-in-law might or might not be at the table. In later years she even had her granddaughters' boyfriends to contend with, finally even great-grandchildren. Somehow, there was always enough, and there was usually something left over. Walk into the kitchen any time day or night and you'd find a couple of leftover biscuits or banana fritters wrapped up on top the stove. In the refrigerator would be a plate of leftover panéed meat or a bowl of vegetable soup.

If you follow these recipes, I can't promise they'll be as good as Grandma used to make, because she never used a recipe. But if you'll pretend there's a short, attentive lady standing right next to you, lifting covers and tasting and saying things like "Watch this don't berl too quick, now" and "Just a tinch more sugar," they should turn out just fine.

Banana Fritters

In this age of natural-everything, there are those who will cry sacrilege at adding unnecessary calories and cholesterol to the already perfect banana. Most of these people were not born and raised in New Orleans where we know God's handiwork can nearly always be improved upon.

Ingredients: 2 cups of flour
1 teaspoon baking powder
1 egg
1 teaspoon vanilla
A little milk (about 1/3 cup)
Ripe bananas

Put all ingredients except milk and bananas in a mixing bowl. Stir in milk until you have a thick batter.

Cut peeled bananas in half and make thick slices, lengthwise. About six slices per banana. Dip bananas in batter. Deep fry until golden brown. Drain on paper towels. Serve sprinkled with granulated sugar as a dessert.

Dixie Beer Bread

There's only one brewery left in New Orleans now and at one time there were dozens. When I was a kid, Dixie called itself The Little Deep South Brewery That Would Rather Be Best Than Biggest. Falstaff was the Choicest Product of the Brewer's Art. Regal Preee-myum Beer and Jax, Mellow Jax are songs that still hum in my head. Now there's only Dixie on Tulane Avenue. The sad truth is that most New Orleanians would rather drink one of those national beers. The tourists ask for Dixie. Even if you don't want to drink a six-pack, here's something that'll make you feel like a solid citizen.

101

Ingredients: 4 cups self-rising flour
4 tablespoons sugar
16 ounces Dixie Beer

Heat oven to 400 degrees.
Grease two loaf pans.
In a bowl, mix flour and sugar, then stir in beer.
The batter will be foamy and lumpy, but don't worry.
Pour it into the loaf pans and bake for 50 minutes.
Brush the tops of the loaves with butter and brown in the oven five minutes more.

Praline Parfait

The hard part about pralines is getting them hard. With this dessert, that problem is circumvented.

Ingredients: 1 cup chopped pecan meat
1 cup brown sugar
1 cup white Karo syrup
1/3 cup water

In a medium saucepan, bring the water to a rapid boil. Add sugar, stirring. Then stir in syrup. Reduce heat.
Cook over medium heat, stirring, until the mixture comes to a boil.
Stir in pecans.
Refrigerate in closed container 3-4 hours until thickened. Spoon over vanilla ice cream.

Calas "tous-chauds"

Here's a hand-me-down Creole recipe you're not likely to find in a restaurant. A long time ago, calas, or sweet rice-cakes, were sold by vendors in the streets like pralines. Since they were best right after they were cooked, the vendors would advertise them as being "all hot." "Calas tout-chauds, madame. Calas tout-chauds." They are delicious.

Ingredients: 3 eggs, beaten
2 cups rice, cooked
1 tablespoon vanilla
1/2 teaspoon salt
1/2 cup sugar
1/2 teaspoon nutmeg
1 cup flour
3 teaspoons baking powder
Milk

Mix all ingredients in a large bowl, adding milk a little at a time to make a thick batter.

Using a large cooking spoon, drop the batter into a pan of hot cooking oil. Turn each cake once.

When cakes are brown, drain them on paper towels and serve sprinkled with powdered sugar.

Bread Pudding with Hard Sauce

Bread pudding is so much a part of growing up in New Orleans that young people who leave home for the first time are astonished to find it in other parts of the world. It is thought to be a local delicacy, like boiled crawfish and Dixie Beer. Made this way it is just that. The only trouble is, there's no way to tell precisely how much you need of the most important ingredient: bread. Grandma Allen would make it when she had about the equivalent of a loaf of french bread, bits and pieces gone stale, in her deep-freeze. Joann and I like to vary our breads, so we'll have a bag of assorted ends and slices in the freezer. When the bag gets full and there's nothing coming up that needs stuffing, it's time for bread pudding!

Ingredients: 6 eggs
      1/2 cup sugar
      1 stick of butter
      1/2 cup raisins
      1 small can fruit cocktail
      1 can condensed milk
      About 1 loaf of stale bread

Sauce: 1 stick butter, softened
      2 cups powdered sugar
      Bourbon whiskey or rum, anywhere from a tablespoon to 1/2 cup. Go for it.

Cream butter and sugar, add eggs and beat.
Mix in raisins, fruit (with juice), and condensed milk.
In a second bowl, soak bread in water until soggy.
Add soggy bread to mixture. Smooosh around with fingers.
Bake at 350 degrees about 45 minutes or until it sets.
For sauce, use butter softened to room temperature, not melted. Work in powdered sugar with fork, add whiskey, stir together, and spoon over hot pudding.

Bread pudding with hard sauce turns the staff of life into the stuff of good times. In New Orleans we cook for fun and for fun we eat.

We create our own appliances and utensils, just to have a better time or to cook more at a time. My brother-in-law, Jim Scott, assembled a magnificent crawfish boiler out of what looks like Sherman tank parts. He made a stirring spoon from a small colander and a wheelbarrow handle. He even constructed an oversize set of tongs for manipulating and tasting without going too near the fiery furnace. Watching Jim perspire and curse over that boiler, getting advice and encouragement from his two sons, testing for salinity and pepper, adding the big onion sacks of corn and potatoes at the critical moment, is an experience denied most humans and virtually all non-Louisianans. Cooking demands our every craft, art, and sacrifice. We are judged by the food we prepare.

I'd say more imagination is lavished on food here than anyplace else on earth. Just take my mother, surprised by afternoon visitors. She'll materialize a handsome tray of hors d'oeuvres and wallow in compliments on their appearance and flavor.

When the other guests are gone, the chef reveals her secret: "Chunks of leftover meatloaf with a little chutney and mustard on top."

And there's another famous New Orleans recipe for your collection.

In the pre-war days the alcoholic beverages were of unsurpassed excellence. The Ramos gin-fizz, of sainted memory, the Sazerac cocktail, may it rest in Peace! The absinthe frappé and the absinthe-anissette...The days when fizz was prepared almost as a religious ceremony are over.

— *Lyle Saxon,*
Fabulous New Orleans, 1928

CRAWFISH TOWN

Looking north, walking south
We get around
Hugging mud, claw to mouth
In crawfish town

By the net, by the pail
They bile us down
Sucking head, pinching tail
In crawfish town

Hardshell dumb, seeing red
By the pound
Pinching tail, sucking head
In crawfish town

Many great doors are shut and clamped and grown gray with cobweb; many street windows are nailed up; half the balconies are begrimed and rust-eaten, and many of the humid arches and alleys which characterize the older Franco-Spanish piles of stuccoed brick betray a squalor almost Oriental.

— George Washington Cable,
Madame Delphine, in Old Creole Days,
1879

RED BEANS AND REVERIE

In an old Creole courtyard on St. Ann Street stands a gray-green statue of Père Antoine. He's a man whose name most of us here know, but few of us can say why we do. Some famous old French priest.

Actually, he was Spanish. When he arrived in New Orleans he was Padre Antonio de Sedella and he was not welcome. Padre Antonio, they say, was a commissioner of the dreaded Spanish Inquisition, sent to rid the colony of voodoo, witchcraft, and other repugnant heresies. But the Spanish Governor, Esteban Miró, understood that in Louisiana black magic existed side by side with Catholicism. In the same pew as it were. Miró put the padre on the next ship back to Spain. Or so one story goes.

Father Antonio must have stayed long enough to get New Orleans into his bloodstream. When the Inquisition ended, he came back as a secular priest, quite willing to let the French-speaking people call him "Père Antoine." He built himself a funny wooden hut near St. Louis Cathedral and the Creoles called him a saint.

Back in Spain, his family had a great deal of money, which Père Antoine could tap when he felt the need. One of his duties was to perform weddings and he felt compelled to give the newlyweds a gift by which they might remember him. So he had a special china pattern created in Florence, and a crate of dinner plates in this pattern was shipped to him on a regular basis. Whenever Père Antoine was seen walking in the vicinity of the cathedral with a plate under his arm, everyone knew there was a wedding going on.

He married three daughters of the family on St. Ann

Street and the statue in the courtyard, done two hundred years later by an artist who lives in the downstairs apartment, shows Père Antoine carrying a dinner plate.

That house is owned by a gracious lady, a Creole, to whom such details of history are as necessary as the vetiver fan she keeps on her coffee table, the setting of forks on the left, the weekly conversations with the old lady who weaves baskets out of pine-needles in the French Market.

The way into her home is through the courtyard and up a flight of stairs to the gallery. "I'm glad you found me," she says. "They haven't changed the name of St. Ann Street yet, eh?"

She is aging, but it is not time's passage she regrets, it is the falling away of familiar things, familiar people. A name is sacred and should be changed only for the sake of marriage.

"I understand now they've changed Melpomene." She pronounces it in the French style, *Melpoh-MENH*. French is the reason behind so many New Orleans pronunciations: one hears, for example, "B'GUNdy" for Burgundy Street .

"They've made it *Martin Luther King Junior Boulevard*, eh? Now I was an admirer of Dr. King. He was a great man. But Melpomene was a great muse. And besides, his entire name is far too long for a street sign. They changed the name of *Craps Street*, you know, where the dice game was invented, out on the edge of the swamp. In those days there were so many croaking *crappeaux* — that's frogs, you know."

She is buxom, matronly, but small and pixieish at the same time. Her skin is soft-soft and white-white, as we say around here, the sort of skin that can only be on the very old or the very young. Around the throat are dewlaps, but their presence lends a sort of regal elegance, as Spanish moss

110

lends to oaks. The eyes are dark and deep-set, behind eyebrows and a precise arch of wrinkles, like dough cut with a crimping tool. Creole eyes, 180 degree old stones set in damask. They are the eyes of the ladies in paintings that hang in the Presbytere. Like both my grandmothers' eyes. Her nose is Gallic, fine boned. You could trace that nose back to the Roman Empire.

"The upper story was added on, you know, during the Spanish period. The bottom floor is strictly French colonial. I'm serving red beans and rice. People say I'm famous for it. Actually, it's the only thing I remember how to cook!"

The lady's name (don't suppose she'd mind your knowing) is Evelyn Soulé Kennedy. Though she reveres the memory of her late husband, she does insist on the "Soulé," an old Creole name. She is a lady of letters, having authored the plays and tableaux staged during the city's annual Spring Fiesta for a number of years.

"When I was younger," she says, "there were still a great many people here who spoke English only as a second language — none too well, most of the time. I remember I went to a school for girls to do a reading and was introduced by the principal. She said, 'And now Madame weel execute herself in her own play.'"

Evvy, as she prefers to be called, drinks nothing more potent than Spanish sherry. She serves an excellent beet salad and even better conversation.

"I had an uncle who went down to Grand Isle to recover from a heart ailment," she says. "He enjoyed it so much he stayed there for twenty years. It was lovely then. My family would go there for vacations when I was little. Later on, after the jitneys started running, we would catch one of those to go downriver aways. But before that, the whole family would go across the river to Harvey's Canal, and at 8 a. m.

we'd board a mailboat. Well, that boat would chug and stop and start and chug some more and stop again, down this bayou and up that bayou, until finally we'd get to Barataria Bay. And by the way, we did *not* run into any pirates."

"Then we traveled over land, although it wasn't really land. We had to ride in this dump-cart sort of thing, pulled by a mule. Now, there was a sort of natural causeway there, out to the island, but it was always covered by a few inches of water. I believe that poor old mule must have been the only living creature that could have found its way. If anything ever happened to that mule while we were on Grand Isle, my dear, I expect we'd be there still. The sun was always setting when we arrived, I remember, and it was a beautiful sight over the water."

The red beans and rice were masterfully prepared. As she spooned the beans from a big black pot, Evvy revealed that she'd learned the recipe from her "mammy," the servant lady who'd cared for her and for all the Soulé children.

"Her name was Leonice, but we all called her Neecie. She was a dear. Neecie spoke the *patois*, of course, and very little English. I remember she had trouble, oh, a great deal of trouble, with American names. When an American boy would come calling on any one of us girls, Neecie would simply refuse to learn his name. But if he came more than once, Neecie would just *have* to find some way to identify him so she could gossip about the young man."

"I'll never forget Douglas Nicholls. When he came over, Neecie heard 'Nickels' and from that moment on, she would call him nothing but '*Michié Cinque-sous.*' Another fellow always wore gray pants, so she called him '*Michié Panta-lons-gris.*'"

"But I must tell you, it wasn't only English that gave poor Neecie a hard time. One day we came back home from a visit to relatives and she presented Papa with the card of a gentleman who had come to call. Neecie was most outdone. She did not know who this fellow was, but she suspected him of being an umbrella salesman, because he carried an umbrella. And he spoke horrible French, barely understandable. She refused to let him in."

"Well, my father looked at the card and said, very gravely, 'Next time he calls, Leonice, you may admit him. He is the new French Consul in New Orleans.'"

After supper we step out on the balcony with our coffee. The sounds of the French Quarter at night are starting to pile up in layers. Live music from a nightclub, juke box from a bar, reveling tourists on Bourbon Street, automobiles, the clop-clop of mules pulling their sightseers. Evvy cannot help noticing how the sounds have changed since she bought her house in the old quarter. That was during the depression, when she received an inheritance of four thousand dollars. She put it all into this house and has lived in it ever since. Her hand rests on the wrought-iron railing. She recalls the ironworks on Bayou St. John where it was made. She loves her recollections.

"Neecie," she said, smiling. Another memory has flitted into her head, sweet as the last taste of brandy found at the bottom of a glass you took for empty. "You know, one day we discovered her putting a dollar out of her salary into an envelope. She didn't want to tell us what it was for at first, but finally she admitted that she did this every week. She'd been doing it every week for *thirty years*. 'Ever since my husband passed.' She mailed it to some 'society' in St. Louis where they would pray for her husband's soul.

"'You know,' she said, 'I got to do what I can to keep him in Purgatory, cause if I don't they gonna send him to hell for sure.'"

On the way out, passing the courtyard statue of Père Antoine, we were thinking of Neecie's concern for Eternity. My own family, and others I've known, have always seemed more concerned with that remote and uncertain immensity than with the immediate future. We'd sooner fret about Purgatory than deal with problems of environmental pollution or public education. I don't know why that is and I certainly don't intend to preach about it. I do wonder, though, whether the old Inquisitor likes his statue.

There's another story about Père Antoine and his generosity, told by Benjamin Latrobe in 1820, when the priest was rector of St. Louis Cathedral. M. Latrobe was trying to help a poor Irish woman whose dying wish had been for a fine Catholic burial. Of course her family could not afford the ten-dollar fee for such a service. "I wrote to Père Antoine," said Latrobe, "begging him to diminish the fees as much as possible, and received for an answer that if a dollar were paid to the Sexton he would pay the rest himself."

I walked to the Cathedral to see if there might be a monument erected at the spot where Père Antoine built his ramshackle rectory. There isn't. Sometimes we take our saints for granted.

"One must get acclimated," responded the Creole... "They all do it — all who come. They hold out a little while — a verhy little; then they open thei' sto'es on Sunday, they impo't cahgoes of Afrhicans, they brhibe the officials they smuggle goods, they have colo'd housekeepe's. My-de'-sseh, the wata must expect to take the shape of the bucket, eh?"

*— George Washington Cable,
The Grandissimes, 1880*

faith

ELEMENTARY SCHOOLS
ARCHDIOCESE OF NEW ORLEANS

2nd-8th Gra

40

CHARACTER REPORT

PUPIL'S REPORT

James Major

SCHOOL DAYS 1956-57

CHICKEN DINNER

Given by

High School Parents Club

CAFETERIA

$1.25

Reward of Meri

CERTIFIES THAT

HAS BE

UNCTUAL, DILIGENT AND OBEDIENT

194

FAITH OF OUR FATHERS

Of the two state religions (or reasonable facsimiles thereof) which exist in this country, I am unfamiliar with one. That one is Mormonism, the preferred religion of Utah. My wife went to do a concert in Provo once and they would not let her sing until she promised not to smoke, drink, cuss, or wear a low-cut gown. Those preferring a more tolerant semi-official religion would do well to settle in South Louisiana, where Roman Catholicism makes no such unreasonable demands upon its adherents or guests.

Spiritual control of the early colony was never a question, though middle management seemed unstable from the start. The early church in Louisiana was under the Bishop of Quebec, too far away to exert his authority. Consequently, the Jesuits and the Capuchins argued over jurisdiction of New Orleans, particularly over control of the hard-working Ursuline nuns. When the Jesuits ran into trouble in Europe they were banned from the colony. Later, the Jesuits would return with a vengeance.

In 1762, France gave Louisiana to Spain and Cuban bishops were put in charge. A Spanish diocese was created out of Louisiana and Florida. Thus a territorial battle was joined between the French Capuchins and the Spanish Capuchins. It was during this period that ecclesiastical boundaries were drawn and Louisiana was divided into parishes. These would form the basis for political subdivisions which, in any other state, would have been called counties.

In 1800 Napoleon got Louisiana back for France, creating another episcopal shuffle. Then, three years later,

117

Napoleon sold the whole territory to the United States. That ended the Catholic Church's official hold on Louisiana, but unofficially the struggle for the minds and hearts of its people was just beginning.

Until 1803, it was illegal for Protestants to conduct religious services in Louisiana. If a Protestant had the misfortune to die in New Orleans, he could not be buried in consecrated ground. His body was taken to the "Cemetery of the Heretics." It was not until two years after the Louisiana Purchase that the first protestant church, Episcopal, was founded in New Orleans.

One hundred and fifty years later, when I was a child, it was still an event to discover that someone you knew was a "non-Catholic." One never specified the heresy, never even gave a name to the outsiders, such as Jews confer upon Gentiles. They were not "Baptists" or "Methodists," merely "non-Catholics." We lived in a Catholic World. Our St. Joseph's Missals were dogeared and thumb-printed, our Baltimore Catechisms the products of God's own printing press. My grandmother said her prayers twice each day, kneeling on the *prie dieu* in her bedroom. On WSMB radio you could hear the rosary recited every evening. Riding a bus or streetcar you felt peculiar if you forgot to make the sign of the cross every time you rode in front of a Catholic church. On unfamiliar bus routes I sometimes found myself the lone crosser and would realize, to my profound humiliation, that I had crossed for a *non-Catholic* church. We all believed then that the nuns and priests got their instructions directly from the Pope, who had an audience with Jesus twice weekly. It was a simple faith, an absolute faith, a faith that would admit no doubt. Inevitably, I suppose, doubt crept in anyway. Inevitably, I had to lose my religion to regain my faith. There were two incidents that drove me

118

to heresy.

The first happened Easter morning, 1951. I was eight years old, a communicant of one year. I did not know that Easter had been named after a pagan goddess and that Gene Autry invented the bunny trail. It was Jesus, I believed, who directed the large and unseen rabbit to our house. It was the Holy Ghost who decided how many marshmallow eggs, what color jellybeans, how large a chocolate rabbit each child received. What I did not understand was how God could ordain all these edible miracles — delivered on time, no matter how early I arose to trap the bunny — then turn around and demand total abstinence, just so a kid could receive Communion.

What made matters worse was that, of the five children then in our home, I was the only one old enough to have made my first communion. All the others could with impunity devour half the contents of their baskets before they got dressed for Mass.

Just as we were being herded out the front door toward the car, I realized I didn't have my missal. When I ran back inside to fetch it, I found myself alone in the living-room, alone with the five Easter baskets, alone with all their sweet temptations. I picked up an Elmer's Gold Brick from my own basket, but realized it would leave a tell-tale trail of chocolate around my face and fingers. Besides, someone would notice it had been removed, for sure. The horn of the old Plymouth was blowing outside. I had to make up my mind in a hurry.

My eyes fell on a carton of wax milk bottles, the kind that came filled with sticky, colored syrup. They were in my sister Jeannine's basket. I snatched up a tiny bottle, bit the top off and sucked down the purple nectar. Like the forbidden fruit must have tasted to Adam, nothing before or since has seemed so sweet to me.

It was on the way to St. Francis Xavier Church that the enormity of my crime struck me full in the face. It slammed hard as my sister Melanie's patent-leather pump swinging against my shin. If I stood in line for confession, I would be admitting sin to my mother, who had taken me to confession the day before...even though, I would not actually commit the sin until I let the Lord's body touch my tainted tongue. To sit out communion was unthinkable. I was trapped. I had violated—or was about to violate— the Baltimore Catechism's communion commandment: Thou shalt not eat nor drink anything except water after midnight, before taking Holy Communion.

I could not plead ignorance. I had scored points in catechism class by defending the use of toothpaste, provided one did not brush with the intention of swallowing. I knew exactly what my soul looked like, as illustrated in the Baltimore Catechism. It was a milk bottle, just like those damned wax bottles in the Easter basket. Only now the milk in my soul was spotty because I had failed to avoid the near-occasion-of-sin. It was about to become black as tar, black as Beelzebub's eyeballs. Old Father Miller was mumbling the Latin, as he always did, but the word's pierced my heart: *Domine, non sum dignus.* Lord, I am not worthy.

I walked up to the communion rail behind my father, head bowed, sweating. My collar was tight as last year's underwear. My mother walked on ahead, carrying the current baby, who was named Celeste. I knew Jeannine and Jimmy and Melanie were in the pew kicking and poking each other and I'd have given my entire Easter basket plus the three holy cards I got from winning the March spelling bee, just to be back there in the pew with them. I thought about turning off at the front cross-aisle, but my knees were too weak to do anything but kneel. Mephistopheles was in control.

Father Miller doled out wafers to my mother and father, coming ever closer with his Latin mumble. ("*Tomfy uh-tonnum,*" is what it sounded like.) The fat, hairy fingers were in the golden cup. The white, flat bread that looked like a Necco wafer but was really the Body of Our Lord and Savior Jesus Christ moved toward my outstretched, quivering, syrup-stained tongue. "*Tomfy uh-tonnum*" said Father Miller. "*Domine, non sum dignus ut intres sub tectum meum,*" I told my God, hoping he would understand better than I did.

The communion wafer broke against the *tectum* of my mouth. The evil deed was done. I carried the guilt of that moment the next ten years of my life.

At first the sin was too terrible to confess, then too old — as though there could be a statute of limitations on blasphemy. Finally, I told myself it was all too trivial, all too funny. But I wasn't laughing.

It was at Mass during my sophomore year at Loyola, a noonday Lenten Mass, that the milk bottle of my soul finally broke. I was kneeling in the Byzantine splendor of Holy Name of Jesus Church as a young priest elevated the host, intoning the sacred formula which transformed plain flour and water into the flesh and sinew of the Son of God. My life was in a muddle then, I recall. Writing poetry, fondling breasts, contemplating Nature, and despairing the hypocrisy of my parents' world — these were the ways I wasted my time and their money; I had half a mind to become a Jesuit myself. Then I heard the words again, really listened to them:

"Behold the Lamb of God. Behold Him who takes away

the sins of the world. Lord, I am not worthy that Thou shouldst come under my roof. Say only the word and my soul will be healed."

The young priest was mumbling these words just the way old Father Miller had mumbled. It was all rote, all gibberish. *Tomfy uh-tonnum.* This was *God*, GOD, in his poor, sweaty, dirty human hands. The priest should be orating like Cicero. He should be singing like Caruso. His feet should leave the floor. (I willed him up, levitated him in my mind. But he did not move.) Or he should scream and fall down in a faint.

How could it happen otherwise?

Oh.

The moment numbed my soul. It was all a lie. All the rules, all the guilt, all the pretending. The doctrine of transubstantiation was no more than the doctrine of the Easter Bunny. Tales told to mystify the children and keep them in their places, in their pews.

I took the host that day and chewed it. It was not God, it was bread, as it had been always. I became a heretic.

If I die in New Orleans, they can bury me in the cemetery of the heretics.

EMILE LAILE P. H.

Meaning Professor of Hoodoo
All manner of Hants and Hoodoos removed
with neatness and dispatch.
No witch doctor is too strong
for My power
References exchanged
Special attention to Emergency calls
Office, 2928 Orleans Street
My Office Hours Any Time
All Mail Orders Filled

— business card handed out in 1913,
Reprinted by Robert Tallant, Voodoo in
New Orleans, 1946

To the stranger visiting New Orleans for the first time, one of the most interesting places to see are the cemeteries, from the novelty of their construction, the tombs and vaults nearly all being built above ground in the shape of ovens. This is caused by not being able to dig graves, due to the fact that they become filled with water, caused by the ground, on which the city is built, being lower than the water in the Mississippi River.

— Visitor's Guide to the World's Industrial and Cotton Centennial Exposition, 1884

MISSING LINK

They'll remember a white face, my sisters, my cousins. They'll remember a white face fringed with white stubble. They'll remember wisps of white hair, loose, falling, lost on white pillows and white sheets. Even the eyes they'll remember not blue but milky gray, brimmed with pale tears never quite ready to drop. They'll remember him small, collapsing in on himself like a dead star between those white sheets, or hunched and humbled in his gray wheelchair.

But he was a large man who fit ill between sheets, a man of many deep colors. When he died his children's children numbered thirty-five. His wife, my maternal grandmother, Creole to the marrow, died ten years too early. And she'd been ill, living on memories, years before that. It took that long to drain the color and the size and the life out of my grandfather, I guess.

Among his many grandchildren (some of his children too, perhaps) I knew him best, being the first child of his first child. I saw his colors brightest, his size most grand. Although he was always an old man to me, he helped paint the walls of my child's imagination.

He and my grandmother lived uptown in the Garden District, among the rich, though they were far from rich themselves. My favorite years of childhood were the years when I was old enough to travel from our house in Metairie to their house on Seventh Street, and still young enough to cherish spending a weekend with "Mère and Mash."

My grandmother went about like a grand lady, corseted and lacey, between her bedroom at one end of the apartment and the kitchen at the other. Her bedroom was cool and shadowy, with heavy curtains. There was a vanity, spread with mysterious jars and crystal bottles, a wide mirror above it. There was, on another wall, a *prie dieu* my grandfather had built, its top draped with a heavy black rosary and mysterious little cards, a crucifix above it. There was a dresser with deep drawers she let me rummage in now and then, and I knew if I'd been a girl I'd spend more time there.

The kitchen was a better boy's place, with eternal Zelda, the maid, cooking and washing and ironing, in and out. The radio on a shelf went from one soap opera to the next, their organ themes like a shifting current of melodrama in my head. *And now...The Loves of Helen Trent...which asks the question, can a girl from...Our Gal Sunday...The Love of Life...brought to you by pure, mild Ivory Liquid...stay tuned for the Guiding Light....*

Next to the kitchen was a stairway, which led to the back yard downstairs and the attic upstairs. Mister Henry, the Italian ice man let himself in this way, a fifty-pound block of ice held on his back by long, magical tongs that would lift and hold the ice even when he used just one hand. A burlap rag kept Mister Henry's back from freezing, though his blue shirt was always soaked through. He had a broad open smile and a broad open nose. He whistled as he came up the stairs, carrying the weekly ice to the green metal box on the outdoor landing. I'd go out to meet him and we'd have important conversations.

There was a landing indoors, too, just off the kitchen, where my grandfather kept his tools, his workbench, his lathe. From a high stool in the corner I'd watch, filling my nose with sawdust.

Mash would start with a slice of tree and turn it to a smooth disk swimming with grain. He'd talk about the grain and show me what it meant. He'd screw the wood back on the lathe and start the motor up and select a chisel with just the right curve. Turning, spinning faster and faster, the disk would grow a rim and a base, losing long curls like a baby at his first haircut. Soon I'd know it was becoming a bowl to fill with candy or salted peanuts.

Mère spent time each day on the telephone, slipping in and out of French, heaving her bosom, rolling her wide eyes at some shocking news or other. Mash would come home from the office in his seersucker suit, with suspenders that made the only creases in his starched cuffed shirt. He'd change into his work clothes and we'd go off to do a job together.

On Saturday afternoons we'd sit in the living room and turn on the elegant, highbacked radio, to share the mystery of football. Sometimes it would be Tulane, but it was Notre Dame he loved more, being confirmed Irish. Sitting on the rug I'd watch his face for signals. When to shrug, when to tense, when to cheer. If the game was going badly he'd curse the goddam priests for letting in the goddam Polacks. Later it was the goddam niggers. His prejudices were expansive and generously dispensed.

On three or four occasions we actually went to real football games at Tulane Stadium. The memories soaked in deeper than the damp bleachers etched into my legs. It felt grand sitting beside him, bundled in lap robes, sucking on a Coke as he sucked on a pocket flask, knowing precisely when to cheer, when to tense, when to shrug.

Sleeping in that high-ceilinged house on Seventh Street was wonderful, too. Theirs was only an apartment, the upper story, but it was the most space I'd ever known, the stillest times. Dreams would end in the sound of streetcars rocking by on the St. Charles tracks half a block away.

Mornings broke sometimes with the clopclop of mules' hooves, pulling a garbage wagon or a rag wagon. Still mules, even in those days.

It was Mash who opened the attic door for me the first time and there, for the first time, I saw things past use, past need. In the mirrored front of an old armoire, between the gloss and the reflection, I felt a mist that moved, full of images, lingering shades of souls beyond recall. I saw dress forms of shapes now shapeless, walking sticks of polished wood that had outlived bone. I saw a strange, high chair with back and seat of shredding cane, arms of dark-rubbed pine; in place of legs it had wide iron wheels. My grandfather did not spend much time in that attic and he refused permission for me to go there alone.

Some afternoons I'd meet him downtown at the office building he managed. First it was the Canal Bank Building, later the California Company. He had an office filled with ladies who made much over me. They gave me Cokes and exotic knickknacks from their desk drawers. His secretary asked me once if I knew my grandpa had been a young man on great ships, that he'd been on the first ship through the Panama Canal. I told her no, I didn't know that.

Two or three times, in the fine old DeSoto with its rich tobacco aroma and its custom-installed airconditioner, they took me on long trips. We rode to a great plantation where relatives lived. I tasted wild rice, wild duck, wild goose. I was in a remote place called Crowley.

But it was uptown New Orleans to which my grandparents belonged, among the hoopskirted oaks and wide-lapped houses, among the tilting sidewalks with cracks that fill with acorns and monkeygrass and jasmine, among the black iron fences thick with azaleas. Near the streetcar tracks. Near Scheinuk's Florist, which we could never pass without a retelling of the two bunnies they'd bought me there one Easter that multiplied themselves into extinction on their front porch. Near Mister Moffet's wonderful fountain drug store, where I could run and buy ten comic books with the dollar Mash would give me. I can't go through that neighborhood now without reviving my grand-parents.

Sometime later, on a trip home from New York, it was Thanksgiving. Mère was years gone and Mash was installed in a nursing home where my mother could be near him. I rolled him to the table. He was all white, in a white guyabera shirt that hung on him like someone else's choir robe. There was turkey, which used to be his favorite. He didn't care. I had to look hard to see the old colors, like faint traces of a woman's makeup after it's worn away. They sat me at the head of the table, even though he was there. They made me ask the blessing, though that was always his prerogative. They even gave me the knife to carve the bird. At the far end of the long table the head of the family sat like an old log barely glowing, waiting to be ash.

Suddenly he laughed. It was a joke no one had meant for him, but one that struck him funny. The laugh was like an awful mistake, like a sweet major chord struck acciden-tally by an organist deep in a minor mood. He was as startled as the rest of us, for he'd done away with laughter. He'd put it in his attic, a thing past use, past need. He broke off the laugh, swore at himself, and left us all uneasy through the meal.

Into his room at the home I pushed him, in a gray, high chair of plastic and steel, with gray rubber wound round its wide iron wheels. I pushed him into his faded pajamas, pushed him into bed, between the white sheets. I pressed my face against his white cheek, felt the white stubble and the drooping white moustache, kissed him, and said I would visit him soon.

Instead, I went back to New York and never saw him again.

They buried him in a closed gray coffin. I was a bearer. I placed the last flower upon it before I turned and walked away, trusting that someone would lower him into the clammy earth of Metairie Cemetery, beside my grand-mother.

The old man was gone, taking with him some of the child.

But I still feel him when I go uptown.

Human rights is, of all subjects, the one upon which this community is most violently determined to have no discussion...What, then, will they do with the world's literature? They will coldly decline to look at it and will become, more and more as the world moves on, a comparatively illiterate people...What a bondage it is which compels a community, in order to preserve its established tyrannies, to walk behind the rest of the intelligent world.

— *George Washington Cable,*
  The Grandissimes, 1880

We bulldozed the negroes; we killed the worst of them; we killed carpetbaggers; we patrolled the roads at midnight; we established in many localities a reign of terror. Why? Not to repress or restrict the freedom of the ballot. The Republicans had the niggers, the Carpertbaggers, the federal army and navy united in an effort to crush the white people out of our state. We had only our undaunted hearts and fearless arms to defend our liberty, our property, and our civilization, and we defeated our oppressors with such resources as God and nature had placed in our hands, and we redeemed our state. Stand forth, ye white-livered cowards and recreants who now seek to dodge the responsibility.

— New Orleans States,
Editorial, July 25, 1899

RACE AGAINST TIME

Black people are as integral to our society as clam shells to our highways. And, by whites, taken just as much for granted.

All those billions of shells scooped up from the bottoms of Lake Pontchartrain, Lake Borgne, and Lake Catherine, crushed into concrete, poured into roadbeds: they all were alive once, homes for sweet, plump bivalves with their own gritty character. Only a few people know you can eat those clams, as long as you're careful how you heat them. With a little sauce they make a fine meal. The Choctaws and the other Indians knew that, but the rest of us tend to overlook the finer qualities of Louisiana clams.

For two hundred years or more, the people who called the shots in New Orleans lived in the midst of black people. Instead of discerning their finer qualities, we put up signs like *gris-gris*, voodoo warnings, to keep them out of our places. They couldn't eat with us, drink with us, ride with us, or go to the bathroom with us.

It was on the buses, where you could see its victims, that I learned the most about prejudice. Soon as I was old enough I traveled by myself, often as I could, to my grandparents' house uptown. Took the Metairie line on Metairie Road, changing at the cemeteries to the Louisiana. At St. Charles Avenue I'd transfer to the street car. It was an adventure.

Every bus and streetcar had rows of seats on either side of a center aisle. The back frame of every seat had two holes in it, and into those holes plugged metal pins which supported a wooden sign about two feet wide. The signs were heavily varnished and impressed with the words "Colored Only." According to city ordinances, you were a criminal if you sat on the wrong side of that sign.

Really, it was comical that white folks had got themselves in such a fix. There were no "White Only" signs on the buses. If you got into a bus like the Louisiana Avenue bus, shuttling its cargo of housemaids and mammies between their homes and their jobs, you were likely to find the sign pushed forward as far as it would go. This left precious little room for non-colored passengers.

What's more, those signs were susceptible to kids. Black kids moved them forward, even when there were plenty of good seats in back; white kids moved them back when there was more than enough room up front. We all spent our entire kid lives being told where to sit, in classrooms and churches, at tables and in cars. Even at the movies we couldn't sit in the front rows, where every kid knew he belonged, on account of some blinding agent purported to leap from the screen at close range.

On a bus, the driver was too busy aiming at potholes to keep an eye on kids. Early on I discovered that the best of all possible bus seats was the very last seat that stretched from one side of the bus to the other. There you felt the bumps and swerves more keenly. There you could prop up your feet unobserved. There you could fold up *Rider's Digest* into paper airplanes and fly them out an open window without being caught.

Of course, in that back seat there were no holes drilled for the "Colored Only" sign. At first I solved that problem by propping the sign in the back window. However, that seemed unfair, since it required black people to run behind the bus. Gradually my better nature taught me to ignore the sign altogether. If coloreds were good enough to sit in the back, I reasoned, then I was good enough.

They've written a lot of books and movies about those courageous black people who refused to ride behind the signs. I've never read anything about those brave white kids who refused to ride in front of them.

White people have always been told where to sit in New Orleans, just as black people have. It started when the white Creoles forced the white Yankees to build their own "American Sector" on the upriver side of Canal Street. Irish immigrants got their ghetto around Magazine Street. Germans went upriver. Today we have a Vietnamese ghetto out on Chef Menteur Highway. The creoles, by refusing to mingle with their supposed lessers, gradually lost control of their city. They simply were overwhelmed.

When Storyville shut down, the swollen community of low-lifes moved into the French Quarter. It was perfect, with its narrow streets and convenient balconies, for their activities, ideally suited for vice, crime, and poverty. The Vieux Carre went quickly to seed and the Creoles let themselves be pushed out. Even Esplanade Avenue with its stately homes and gardens was abandoned. I remember attending a Christmas party at the old family home of a member of a very old Creole family. I was astonished to learn that such gentility ever had existed on a street so seedy as Esplanade. I learned later that my father had been raised just a few blocks away. I assumed that the Creoles of New Orleans had always lived "uptown" — in the American Sector.

When the displaced Creoles began buying up the American homes, the Yankees (they quickly became *nouveau-Creoles*) built even nicer homes across the Parish line in Jefferson. Today the small number of Creole descendants and other whites left uptown fight the ongoing battle for territory with black people, poverty, and crime. They are far outnumbered in the city by blacks, who run the place and who have to figure out what to do about the criminals. People who make money from tourism do battle with gays for control of the French Quarter.

All of which goes to show that signs won't keep anybody in his or her place forever. Even the bus signs were eliminated in 1954 by federal proclamation.

Today you have to marvel at the stubbornness of white supremacists in New Orleans. Here we are, all history and habit, and none of it could have happened without black people. They are integral to our juiciest episodes: plaçage and *Place Congo*, voodoo and the quadroon balls, and the Civil War and Storyville. Our entertainment and tourist attractiveness could be written off without the black people who gave us Dixieland jazz and tapdancing in the streets. Except for our architecture (imported from Europe) and our Mardi Gras (conceived by a bunch of swells from Mobile, Alabama), all we have to brag about is our cooking. And how many of those fine white Creole ladies do you suppose did their own cooking?

I'm always surprised by racism. Naive, I guess.

It wasn't really till I started college, along with the first group of black undergraduates accepted in our chief religious institute of higher learning, that I felt real racism. I mean the kind that stems from deep fears and makes a man burn with shame at his brothers. Later, as a newspaper reporter, I learned a lot more about it. Firsthand. I covered school desegregation in lower St. Bernard Parish and voter registration in Franklin, Louisiana. I interviewed the Grand Dragon of the Ku Klux Klan and shook hands with the black soul of white bigotry, Judge Leander Perez. I learned what it was that made Martin Luther King Jr. so angry.

You see, growing up I'd had no idea about all that. My parents hid it from me, taught me "nigger" was a bad word used by "common" people. If my grandfather slipped into it now and then and my friends' parents peppered their conversation with it, it was just because they were from older generations who never learned any better. So my parents taught me. This was the kind of trivial bigotry you could smile at, no more embarrassing than a burp that came up when you swigged a Big Shot Creme Soda. It took me a long time to understand that our kind of bigotry could be even worse, because it was harder to point a finger at than the other kind.

Got a pet dyed chick one Easter. Somehow it survived its coat of green paint and my mishandling and started to grow up. We weren't allowed real pets around my house, on account of all the children, so you had to make do with the occasional goldfish won at a ring-toss game at the St. Francis Xavier penny-party, or a box turtle Uncle Milo found out by the Indian Mounds. Not since the multiplying bunnies I'd had when I was still an only child had I owned a real warm-blooded animal.

Nobody bothered about my chick until it got big enough to flap out of its shoe box and started dropping its little calling cards around the house. Exile to the back yard worked until the bird achieved health-hazard status by becoming a rooster and waking up the baby sister. My mother said this would give the baby colic. When the rooster pecked me on the hand, my mother took this as incontrovertible evidence that it was destined to put somebody's eye out.

To hold the power of putting out an eye was to be taboo. Blacklisted. Anathema. My mother had banished b. b.

guns, slingshots, oversharp pencils, pocket knives, toy arrows, rocks, and sticks for this same offense. The rooster had to go and I knew it.

George, the black man who took care of our yard until I got old enough to mow, told my mother that his family sure would enjoy having that rooster and he'd be glad to take it off our hands. To keep peace in every place but his son's heart, my dad gave the rooster to George.

I decided, at first, that black children either had tougher eyes or laxer rules. Then, some time later, I understood. George took that rooster home to *eat* it.

For a while, every black person I met was suspect, a potential devourer of pet animals. That's how easy it is to tar a whole group with the same brush, especially when their skin happens to be dark already. On the other hand, it is my experience that black people are just as likely to make snap judgements about us as we make about them. This should be small consolation to any of us.

At my grandparents one day I walked too far toward the river on Seventh Street and got myself into one of those uncertain blocks between distinctly white and for-sure black homes. There I met a boy about my age who said his name was Jerome.

My friend Jerome had a yo-yo I much admired and I showed him how to walk the dog with it. He said he'd be willing to part with that yo-yo for three D-C comics. I invited him to my grandmother's house to wrap up the exchange, but he had to check with his mom and it was getting on to lunch time. We agreed to meet at the same spot after lunch.

Mère, my grandmother, was mildly interested in my having met another "little boy" in the neighborhood, but this news captivated her maid, Zelda. From the kitchen, where

Zelda was stuffing crawfish heads and listening to "Helen Trent," the maid called, "I ain't nevuh seen no chirrun in *dis* neighb'hood, Miz Lynch."

My grandmother caught her drift. She asked me what this little boy looked like. I told her Jerome was colored.

"Ah mighta knowed it," Zelda said, ostensibly to herself. "Ah mighta knowed."

I decided I mighta knowed too. After lunch I went to tell Jerome he couldn't come over. My grandmother had even nixed the trade. Jerome said that was all right because his mother had laid down the law against trafficking with white children. We were victims, not so much of prejudice as of racial resignation. Like high water and hurricanes, there just wasn't anything you could do about a person's skin.

Much later, when I was seventeen, I was asked to take the car and give a lift home to Dorothea, my mother's maid, who was feeling poorly. Since Dorothea was a lady, I showed my breeding by opening the front door of the car for her.

"Honey, I can't ride in that front seat," she said.

"Sure you can. Get in."

"Lawd, lawd," Dorothea said, shaking her head. "What would people think o' that?" She laughed and began to open the rear door.

"I don't care what they think," I said. "Sit up here in the front. Times have changed."

She looked at me hard and there was venom in her voice.

"No they ain't. An' I ain't no fool as to ride in a car with a white boy, sittin' in the front seat. Not in your neighborhood and not in mine."

She got into the back of the Buick and I drove her home.

140

Neither of us spoke. On the way back to my house I felt tears in my eyes and I was ashamed.

*In the shimmering crescent of the great river
is rising a new city, a city packed with marvels
a-plenty to applaud the ancient wisdom of
Indian settlers who named the original site
Tchoutchouma "the place of the sun."... New
Orleans is all things to all men. She provides a
spicy seasoning according to taste. Perhaps it is
all because of the gumbo Nouvelle Orleans, or
the Association of Commerce, or the galvanic
civic spirit, or the old habit of giving lagniappe
to customers, or a combination of all these pleas-
ant solvents of perplexing problems — but
whatever the ingredients or their proportions in
her success, New Orleans has contrived to find
a place in the sun.*

*— Merle Thorpe, "The New New Orleans,"
Nation's Business, January, 1927*

GRAND OPENING
OF THE CHARLES KELLER III
WORLD OF PRIMATES
AT THE AUDUBON ZOOLOGICAL GARDENS

The day they set ol Frankie free
it was somethin to see, somethin to see.
Spent the best of his life,
last seventeen years,
without no grass,
without no tree.
Behind bars ain't no way
for a red-headed stud from Sumatra
to spend his day, I'll say.
I watched him stretch those long arms out
to feel the sun on every hair.
Shook out his burlap sack to shade
his head from the noonday sun.
Mama made it first, his old lady,
found her a place in the roots of
that big grandaddy oak and settled in.
The mayor was goin on about life cycles,
environments, habitats and such hullabaloo
and I remember, in the crowd, seein you.
You had a dreamsicle meltin on your
pink little hand, had to stand
and wait for hizzoner to cut the ribbon.
I wanted to keep them out, all but you,
wanted to take those old bars, old cages,
wanted to put them where that ribbon was.
Then Frankie let out a whoop and ran
across the grass and slapped his hand
against the ship's line, thick as your thigh,

143

and he started to climb and he started to swing
and he started to wave and he started to sing
and he made that sack an orangutan flag
and Mama shook her head at the gag
and the mayor sheared and the crowd cheered
and you were standin next to me
the day they set ol Frankie free.

AUDUBON SOCIETY

The zoo in Audubon Park was one of childhood's chief delights. Stroll through those high iron gates, popcorn in one hand and parent in the other, and you were transported to another world. It was a magical world, a bestiary of wild things that would devour you in an instant but for the maze of bricks and bars that held them back. It was, however, a crowded and cramped place. There were always wet spots on the cement floors. There was the rich odor of decay. But you could laugh at the pacing yellow polar bear. You could throw peanuts at the moatbound rock of sweltering monkeys.

By the late 1960's a half-century of benevolent neglect had about killed Audubon Zoo. Cages were rusting. The budget was cut to the point where zookeepers had to beg stale bread and garbage from restaurants to supplement the thousand dollars a month they were given to feed the animals. Humane groups set up picket lines. Some citizens demanded improvements, others insisted on improving human living conditions first.

"How can you air-condition the polar bear when poor folks a few blocks away are dying from the heat?" they demanded. "How can you beautify a monkey house when right next door people on welfare live in shanties?"

It was a very close thing and it was a ten-year battle. Some say the animals won, some say the people won too. I can't think of another instance in the town's long history when private and public citizens worked so hard against such big odds to achieve something as grand as the Audubon Zoological Gardens.

145

Thiry-odd years ago I had my picture snapped by a grinning little man named Meyer Tischler. I was sitting on Mr. Tischler's stuffed zebra near the zoo entrance. The snapshot, taken on Mr. Tischler's home-made box camera and developed on-the-spot in a pan of chemicals, cost my mother thirty-five cents. Today the zebra's gone, replaced by a bear whose bald spots are patched with carpet scraps. But Mr. Tischler's still at the zoo, near the elephant rides, and he'll snap you with his Polaroid for three dollars.

There aren't many other reminders of the old zoo left. A few WPA buildings, vined and respectable, the sea-lion Parthenon, much rejuvenated, the high iron gates, the popcorn in red-and-white boxes. Not much else. A child's experiences at the zoo today, like everything in a child's life today, are more complicated than they were thirty years ago.

Early one morning on the African savannah, my two-year-old daughter and I watched the red-necked ostriches mate.

The female began the flirting, wiggling her brown wings and strutting in a come-hither way. The male, with his distinctive long red neck, fluttered his gray feathers with excitement.

From his perch on a low-slung oak branch a few yards away, a ground hornbill cocked his head and watched, amused.

The female gracefully lowers her body to the ground. Just as gracefully, the larger male settles astride her, stretching his wings to their full ten-foot spread. They seem large enough to let him fly, but they aren't. Yet in coition he moves like an eagle soaring, in the dim memory of flight. Those huge, heavy wings beat the air and stir dust from the earth. Their feathertips flutter independently, like fingertips groping, grasping. The great, pulsing neck swings side to

146

side, like a pendulum in an ever-widening arc. The small, intense head bends lower and lower, scraping the wings, finally slapping against his bare flanks. Just as it seems his neck will snap, it straightens and the two birds give one shudder. It is done.

The voyeur hornbill hopped from its branch and went about its work. The male ostrich rose, then the female. They never uttered a sound.

You could not have had an experience like that at the old zoo.

Later that day, on the elevated path between North and South America, we stopped to watch two slick rodents swim below us. We heard a chubby girl, six years old with blonde ringlets and a T-shirt labeled "Raceland," ask her mother what those two animals were.

"Dat dere's water rats, chere," said the mother.

A little black boy with short pants and wrinkled-down socks disagreed. "No dey ain't. Mah sistuh say dey's *noo-chas.*"

Soon the white family from Cajun country was deep in conversation with the black family from uptown New Orleans. Weren't nutrias and water rats really the same and wasn't the weather fine and wasn't the zoo so nice now.

Only when they walked away did I have the heart to show my Lauren Beth the placard that identified the South American rodents as capybara.

About a thousand years before Christ, a Chinese philosopher named Chuang-tze observed that when people of different backgrounds and classes come together in a zoo, the variety of animal life seems to diminish the differences among human beings. "In the Age of Perfect Virtue," wrote Chuang-tze, "men lived in common with the birds and

147

beasts, and were on terms of equality with all creatures as forming one family. How could they know among themselves the distinctions of superior men and small men?"

As we left the zoo that day, our path again crossed that of the family from Raceland. The father was asking his daughter about her favorite experience at Audubon Zoo. The blonde-curled girl didn't hesitate. "That li'l boy. The one who said them water rats was nutrias."

AUDUBON PARK

When we were young and spring came along,
Foregoing our classes and just for a lark,
We'd cross over St. Charles to Audubon Park.

Bye, bye the bayou banks where the aimless current
Conveyed its drakes to their coy curled-feathered dams,
There we'd lie, sigh by sigh,
Measuring clouds that wandered by,
My fingers opening windows in your hair for the breeze.

There beneath the ambivalent oaks
In their Spanish moss beards and green lichen cloaks
We'd stay by the hour to kindle the spark
That smoldered to love in Audubon Park.

When we were young on warm summer nights,
My Dad's Chevrolet seemed secure in the dark
From the eyes of the world in Audubon Park.

Bye, bye deserted drives where the sleeping golfcarts
Replaced their currents for the day's high-stockinged
  gams,
There we'd cope, grope by grope,
Extracting love from the loins of hope,
Your fingers opening windows in my heart for the wind.

There in the tent of the turbaned night,
Till the leering police brought their lecherous light,
You, Cleopatra supine in her barque,
No mere girl in a car in Audubon Park.

Now in the wisdom of winter, again
In gray-curtained drear, burnt sere and stark
We yearn for the shelter of Audubon Park.

Why, why those churning legs race the aimless current
Past the worried oaks and stone-cold clouds
We cannot say, dare not try.
Is it time so changed, or you and I,
Our fingers locked together against the gale?

There within the great elm cleft
Our eyes fall upon the one gnarled trace we left:
A carved initialed heart to mark
The site of love's temple in Audubon Park.

The alien races pouring into old New Orleans began to find the few streets named for the Bourbon princes too strait for them. The wheel of fortune, beginning to whirl, threw them off beyond the ancient corporation lines, and sowed civilization and even trade upon the lands of the Graviers and Girods. Fields became roads, roads streets. Everywhere the leveler was peering through his glass, rodsmen were whacking their way through willow-brakes and rosehedges, and the sweating Irishmen tossed the blue clay up with their long-handled shovels.

— George Washington Cable,
Jean-Ah Poquelin, in Old Creole Days,
1879

151

Miss Mamie Smith

...ea St. between Magazine & Constance St.

City

THIS SIDE IS FOR THE ADDRESS.

...al Church--Pass Christian, Miss.
..., Pass Christian, Miss.

The cosiest place along the beach
Iz on your lap, my darling peach.

SUMMERHOUSE

A great part of the world assumes that New Orleans, surrounded by water, is *on* the water. They assume we walk down the nearest street and find a beach, like you do in St. Petersburg, Florida, or in Ocho Rios. In fact, now that Lake Pontchartrain — largest in the U. S. except for the Great Lakes — has turned vile, there is no nearby beach for bathing.

New Orleanians have always escaped the city in the summer, provided they had the means. Some, like the Soulé family, went to Grand Isle on the Louisiana Coast. But for many of us, for the last five generations at least, summer escape has meant the Mississippi Gulf Coast. Most particularly the nearby towns of Waveland, Bay St. Louis, and Pass Christian.

Pass Christian, on the eastern lip of the Bay, was an Indian spa before the white men ruined the neighborhood. Into the Twentieth Century there were still a few Indians there, doing business at the old stands, in fruit and vegetables, baskets and pottery. The composer Louis Moreau Gottschalk went there with his family as a child in the early 1800s. Back then the Pass provided escape from the annual summer scourge of yellow fever in the filthy city. Much later, my mother spent her childhood summers in Pass Christian, in a rambling screened home her father built, half a block from the beach. She and her friends were courted there, by their New Orleans beaux who'd come over to spend weekends. When the boys left, the girls would cut their favorites' initials in adhesive tape and plaster them on their skin, creating suntan tattoos.

153

In the early fifties, as soon as my father had anything near the money it took, he found a house in the Pass to rent for the summer. It was on the end of the same street, Sherman Drive, where the house my grandfather built still stood.

Now, Pass Christian is not part of William Faulkner's Mississippi, nor of Willie Morris's. Those delta places are on some other planet from the Gulf Coast. The Coast is, or was then, a suburb of New Orleans, the way Easthampton is a suburb of New York City. There was no literary mystique to be found in Pass Christian, no Snopses and such. It was just a little resort town, with a little church and a little harbor and a little yacht club. It had little identity of its own outside of supplying the needs of the summer visitors from New Orleans, some of whom owned the gracious shady homes with their verandas facing the ocean.

Yet for all its being such an extension of New Orleans, there was distance enough to stretch the umbilical cord thin. That first summer in Pass Christian was the start of my break with childhood, the first step towards the distance I would one day put between myself and the city of my birth. I can see that summer today clear as a ridge in time.

It was the house down by the railroad tracks, still there, set way back from the beach. Probably that's what made it affordable for my dad. It was large enough to hold the nine or ten of us there must have been at that time. But the house was not nearly so large as it seemed, with its wide and welcoming screened porch along the front.

There were four sleeping rooms, plus a little garage apartment out back for Grandmama. Since I was getting too big to sleep with sisters, I only had to share a room with my brother, Jimmy. My parents had the best room, the room where the breeze came in, the room with the old cane-blade ceiling fan that went *ooosh-ooosh-ooosh* all night long.

I remember asking how come Jimmy and I couldn't have that cool room. "Because all your sisters would be jealous," my mom answered. So I asked how come the girls didn't get it, since there were more of them than of anybody else. "Because then you and Jimmy would be jealous," my dad said. It probably never occurred to them that kids can be a whole lot more jealous of their parents than they are of each other.

The sound of the ceiling fan was not the only sound of those Pass Christian nights.

The summerhouse, as I said, was at the end of the street, which dead-ended at the Southern Railways tracks. The train tracks in this part of the country are built up on little levees, on account of all the water. Railroad hills were the only hills I knew as a child, not counting "monkey hill" in Audubon Park.

These Pass Christian tracks were busy tracks, a main route for freight and passengers traveling between New Orleans and points east and north. Three times a day and once each night the trains came growling and roaring and shaking down those tracks, maybe thirty yards from our bedroom. Three times a day and once a night, unless he was down at the beach or off somewhere else, my brother Jimmy would suffer a conniption fit over those trains.

At the first low distant whistle, Jimmy's eyes would bulge and well with tears. He'd start to shiver. His thick and curly blond hair, the only hair like that in the family then, would straighten and go dark like a sponge from the sudden rush of sweat. He'd start wailing and then he'd hoot. By the time the train got to us Jimmy'd be making more noise than the train was. He'd be under a bed or in a closet or behind a dresser, whichever happened to be handiest for hiding out.

Jimmy was scared witless by those trains.

Could be it was something worse than trains. Could be my little brother was suffering what Carl Sagan says is every mammal's instinctive terror of dinosaurs, the "dragons of Eden." Whatever was tearing through Jimmy's soul, the rest of us didn't understand it. Mostly we other kids laughed, and my mother lost her temper more than once.

After a couple of weeks I began feeling sorry for the little guy. I'd climb under the bed with him or join him hunched over in the closet and try to make it into a game for him. A kid can stand anything if it's got fun in it. Even rollercoasters and 3-D horror movies.

He finally came around and played with me. We'd pretend the train was a spaceship from Mars coming to save the Earth or it was a volcano erupting and we had to get away in our speedboat or it was Sitting Bull and ten thousand screaming Indians and we had to get the wagons in a circle quick. In situations like that, Jimmy trusted me. He had seen me in action back in New Orleans and would have given his best cap pistol and his scruffy old cowboy boots for a chance to get in on one of those big-guy games.

After that first summer, Jimmy's dragons went away. It was like he'd never given trains a second thought. He started annoying me by tagging along to pick blackberries by the tracks or to lay pennies along the rails to get them squooshed. I got to wishing I'd left him under the bed.

Unlike Jimmy's, my own first feelings toward trains never changed. I loved those tracks by the summerhouse, loved to watch the trains. Sometimes the engine would be a huge old pufferbelly, iron pistons pushing like a giant's arms. Sometimes it would be diesels, linked back to back like great mechanical junebugs. They seemed almost as tall as the building where my grandfather worked. Boxcars, coalcars, tankcars, cattle cars with their blurred smells. They rocked by in parades a mile long and I'd make bets with myself on whether or not there'd be a red caboose at the end. Generally, there was.

When the trains weren't there, the rails and crossties provided entertainment. A boy could balance barefoot on the slick-worn steel and feel trains long gone or trains yet to come. A boy could sit cross-legged on the ties, watching a cricket or a grasshopper or a monstrous devilhorse. He could spend a half-hour pitching gravel, searching the distant bend near Henderson Point with a wary eye for the single, rolling light of the engine.

Some days I woke too early for any of the other kids on the street and I'd walk along the far side of the tracks, where fields and woods began, and I'd hunt the ditch weeds for just-bursting berries that ran purple down my chin and chest.

And for all the sheer delights of those tracks, it was what lay at the other end of Sherman Drive we'd come to Pass Christian to find.

The beach. The longest manmade beach in the world, my dad said. Not a white beach, parched and lifeless, but a wide expanse of warm yellow sand. Gold-dust dropped from the sun. It teemed with the million tiny wet invisible lives that kept the grains in constant motion.

It was the beach that drew us to Pass Christian. The beach with its low lapping surf. The beach with its gentle staired seawall. The beach with its hundred ribs of bareplanked piers built high on creosote pilings. Those piers made straight the rich folks' path over the heads of us in the merely privileged middleclass. But they could make shade for the lowliest from the noonday sun, and no boy of my acquaintance ever was impeded by a pier's locked gate.

157

Much as I loved the water, it was the beach that gave me the greatest pleasure. I could, still can, fill hours in amazement at the malleability of that wide yellow beach. I sat for days on end, a Titan child, molding the earth into my design.

My mother, I know, taught me the secrets of sand castles. Clear as this morning's breakfast is that moment in my memory. Her bathing suit, it was red and polkadotted, had a modest ruffle around the bottom.

She showed me the way of scooping out a handful of sand from over here and depositing it over there. "You can't rush sand castles," she told me. When she let fall a handful of new sand on the small mound we'd made I was disappointed. Most of the handful trickled down. It wouldn't stick to the top. "Wait," she said. "A little stayed on the top. The rest makes our sand castle wider. If it's wider, there's more top to stick to."

Even Herman Melville would flinch at the symbolism you could draw out of that, I guess. But it's how my mother taught me to build sand castles. The droppings of today are the foundations of tomorrow. And that's how all my dreams and stories have grown, come to think of it.

She was slender then, in spite of all the children, with legs that seemed so long, but which never seemed to tan. She told me I could fill the moat with water from the sea.

At first I'd tote it up from the shoreline in my pail or in someone's discarded Nehi bottle. It was my father who showed me how to draw the water from the sand. "It's right down there," he said, "if you dig deep enough."

My father taught me how to find the wet-wet sand, how to fill my fist with oozing muck and squeeze it out slow like icing from a baker's funnel. Thanks to him my castles had spires like the swirls of Dairy Queen cones, embankments

158

and ramparts lined with boulders, and pyramided fir-trees, all cast from the globby wet sand.

I know to this day there's no place like a beach for dreaming. A beach has its dawn dreams, its morning dreams, and its midday dreams. It has its lazy afternoon dreams and whisper-still evening dreams. It has its long, cool night dreams, too, after a boy's old enough to be out there under the stars by himself, and those are among the best. A beach has its winter dreams, blanketed in chill folds of fog that turn a man in on himself. And winter dreams are good.

I know this, also: that beach in Pass Christian's as much a part of my New Orleans as the streetcar I rode on Canal Street to high school. You can call it Mississippi if you want to, but I think that's a mistake.

FEAR ACHIEVERS

Hermit crabs on welfare waiting
Line the jetty at late low tide.
Live so good in gummint housing,
Need so little on life's free ride.
Talkin's cheap and plenty of it —
Out the window, sidewalk stoop,
Barstool pile —
"You seen that woman?"
"Got bad crack."
"Heard bad soup,
Campbell's can.
Done tried to wear it."
"Sharp as razorclams, tin lids."
"Woman's place be in the conch shell."
"Now who gonna raise them kids?"
...Worry experts. Fear achievers.
No love lost by hermit crabs.
"Whatchew think that gull be up to?"
"Last one outside's up for grabs."
Wear your fort, the world's your oyster.
Give that shell-shocked style a stab,
Lock your doors and bar your windows,
Be a happy hermit crab.

160

*While we're young
and the spring is sprung, let's go moonlight
strollin',
'cause once you're old
and the blood gets cold, no more rockin' and
rollin'.*

— *Little Willy John,
While the Rockin' Is Good*

No place like a beach

GRAND ISLE
"THE ISLE OF ENCHANTMENT"
——For——
Pleasure, Relaxation and Health

ROCKACHAWS

The rented summerhouse made my folks so happy that after a couple of years they bought a place in Pass Christian. It was on the same street, only closer to the beach, right next door to the house my mother's father built, though it was a long time since anyone from our family had owned a place there.

The street was thick with kids, infants on up to teen-agers. The bestlooking one was Butsy Renard's big sister, Connie. You could hide up in the branches of the big mulberry tree that overhung the street between our house and the Renards' and get a real good peek into Connie's cleavage as she walked up from the beach in one of those little two-piece suits she wore.

One day Butsy and I were sitting on the seawall, staring at Connie and two of her friends sunning themselves out on the beach. Connie had her top untied, I could tell that even from a distance. Butsy was pulling a rockachaw out of his toe.

Now, if you don't know what a rockachaw is, it's a whole lot easier to draw one than to try to describe it. A rockachaw looks like

that. They favor the sandy soil right along the coastline. In fact, I've never seen their like anywhere else. When they're young and green, the spikes bend underfoot and feel no worse than soft pebbles. But when the burr matures it hardens into a ball of spines that seem to be tipped with tiny barbs. Those spines go in your skin at every crazy angle and refuse to come out. They hurt like the dickens. Don't confuse them with those merely irritating little sticker-burrs that cling to your pants and Pekingese dogs in high grass. Those things are pansies next to a patch of rockachaws.

Butsy Renard went to St. Stanislaus school, over in Bay St. Louis, where the rockachaw is their emblem — I don't suppose you can call it a mascot. The St. Stanislaus Rockachaws. If that isn't stupid I don't know what is. Butsy claimed it had something to do with the teachers being "so daggone agg'avatin'," but I didn't believe that.

Anyway, Butsy was pulling this rockachaw out of his toe and I was squinting at the three girls on the beach when I said, "I sure wish that sister of yours would stand up right now."

"How come?" asked Butsy, rhetorically. "Wanta see her daggone titties?"

As I answered, Connie did sit up, holding her top and somehow managing to tie the strings behind her back at the same time. How do you suppose a girl learns to do that?

"I can fix it so you can see the whole daggone thing."

"You mean...?"

But there was no time to elaborate. The three girls — women to me — were gathering up their beach towels, radios, suntan lotion, and arcane paraphernalia. "Come on," Butsy said, leaping over the rockachaw patch into Highway 90. "We gotta beat 'em home."

Butsy's pleasure-dome was the bathroom laundry bin, the *dirtyclothes* we called it. Like the one in our bathroom in Metairie, the Renard dirtyclothes had a wicker-mesh

164

trapdoor, about waist high, that pulled down on hinges to let you heave stuff in. The bin was just barely wide enough to hold two boys. The light inside was dim and the air was close.

"Here," whispered Butsy, shoving a handful of dirty laundry into my hands. "You gotta cover your head in case they open up the door. And you gotta be quiet."

I crouched there next to Butsy, covered with somebody's underwear and socks, waiting to be thrilled. Looking through the wicker trapdoor was like a priest's view through the confessional grill.

Eavesdropping was a favorite hobby of mine. I'd logged dozens of late-night hours lurking in the hallway, peeking around a corner into the living room of our Metairie house. I hoped to catch my parents at something suspicious, but they only watched television. I guess television was still a big novelty in those days. I wonder how they had all those children, though, concentrating so hard on *Amos 'n Andy* (sponsored by Kirschman's Furniture Store, three-oh-six-oh Dauphine Street, the place where friendly shoppers meet) and *Boston Blackie* (Brought to you by Bardahl. Use Bardahl in your car and never fear. I never feared.)

We tensed as we heard the three girls approach the bathroom. Connie, the buxom, kinky-haired blonde. Louise, the lanky, pouting brunette. Margie, the little sandy-haired girl. Butsy knew all their names and detested them equally as I adored them all. Butsy was a year younger of course.

The girls crowded into the bathroom, talking all at once, the way girls do, shaking their hair out, the way girls do. Through the confessional grill we could see and hear it all. I hardly knew where to set my eyes... and they still had their suits on.

Louise said, "I need a clean towel," and I knew the golden moment was at hand. The suits were about to come off.

"Give me that sandy one," Connie said, moving toward our bin. Butsy gulped audibly and pulled me lower, down on top of him.

The trapdoor opened. Wet, sandy towels plopped onto my head and back. They felt awful.

"You can throw your suits in here too, if you want," Connie said. "My mom'll wash 'em."

The wet bathing suits covered the towels, but I didn't mind. As soon as Connie closed that trapdoor I'd be staring at heaven. Three naked girls.

Women are given too much credit for attention to details. Find a job with a lot of details and somebody says, like it's gospel, "That'd be a good job for a woman." Well, it's not true. Women will invariably fold hand towels in half when it's obvious as can be they won't hang right unless they're folded twice. They leave lights on and doors unlocked.

Just like Connie Renard left that trapdoor open.

It was Paradise out there and we needed a peephole, not a wide-open gate. We'd be exposed if we so much as lifted our heads. Still, since they'd be exposed too, I was tempted. Butsy's scrawny knees in my chest were another temptation. But there are times a spy blows off an assignment so as not to blow his cover. There was no telling how many times we could play this game without being discovered, so long as we were patient. Besides, the conversation took an interesting turn. Margie was talking about "going all the way."

"I'll bet you never did," Louise said.

Margie laughed a sly, sophisticated laugh she'd picked

up from some movie.

"If you're so hot, Margie," — this was Connie talking — "you better meet those guys from Keesler with us tonight."

"What guys?"

"Guys," Louise said.

"*Big* guys," said Connie. She and Louise giggled, conspiratorially.

"They're drivin' down from Biloxi to meet us on the beach tonight. Wanna *come?*" Another giggle.

Margie demurred. Her mother said she had to be home by nine. You could hear in her voice they'd called her bluff. They knew it, I knew it. Probably even Butsy down on the floor knew it.

By this time the three girls were heading out to the hair dryers, my plan was formulated. Butsy and I would be there tonight, when the big guys from the Air Force base showed up. It promised to be an even better show than the one we missed.

If your timing was right you didn't need a whole lot of permission to go out after dark at the Pass. Volunteering to do the dishes was a sure way to avoid objections to "going out for a while" afterward. It also guaranteed the absence of tag-along siblings. I washed dishes in record time that night, then left them to dry in the sink. I met Butsy in the old chicken coop behind his house. He was blustering about maybe snitching on his sister, but I talked him into waiting . "You got three choices if you hold off," I said. "First, what goes on tonight might be so much fun you want to see it again. Second, if nothing happens you can tell on Connie later and count on her getting punished a whole lot worse for doing it than for just thinking about it. Or third — and even better — you could hold it over Connie's head by *threatening* to tell, and making it sound a whole lot worse than it really was. All in all, you got nothing to gain by telling your mom now."

Butsy saw the sense in that argument, so we hustled down to the old garage at the Gaudin place, a house fronting the beach that was nearly always deserted. The rest of the property was kept up by a yard man, but nobody ever got around to fixing up that garage. It was peeling and dilapidated, with vine-covered, cracked window panes that afforded a good view of Sherman Drive. We took turns, one of us keeping watch from a post on the back fender of an old rusty Packard, the other nosing around the junk in the garage. An archaeological dig.

I was contemplating an ancient and enormous brown bottle labeled "Freund's Family Liniment. Apply Freely Without Rubbing. For Man or Beast" when Butsy called my attention to the fact that he could stand on the Packard's bumper and pee through a hole in the garage door. I admired his aim but told him the noise of the stream hitting the dry leaves outside was unacceptable.

"Daggone," he whispered suddenly. "They're here."

I knew that once it started, pee was hard to shut off. There was nothing to do but wait helplessly while the girls walked by, floppy sandals clicking on the asphalt. "Sssssss," went the leaves. (I was reminded of that oft-cited bestseller, *The Golden Stream* by I. P. Freely, companion volume to *Antlers in the Treetop* by Whogoose de Moose.) But the girls went by, whispering, giggly, and oblivious to any conspiracy save their own.

As soon as Butsy finished relieving himself we went after them, dodging the wet leaves. Outside it was almost completely dark now and the two girls, flopping down the incline and across Highway 90, were silhouetted against the southern sky. They walked toward a fat, sleek Chevrolet in the parking bay across the road. Two guys got out to take their hands as Connie and Louise reached the seawall.

Butsy and I hid behind an oleander bush in the Gaudin's front yard, a good hundred and fifty feet from the action. We saw some fairly involved kissing, and we could tell this was not the first meeting between the boys and the girls. They got some things out of the car and sat on the seawall, hidden from us by the Chevrolet.

"Daggone," said Butsy. "What now?"

"We've gotta move under the car," I answered.

"Kick off your daggone shoes then. Too much noise."

Butsy, as always, was barefoot. He'd spent his entire career on the Gulf Coast, after a brief infancy in New Orleans, and his feet were hardened against anything man or nature could set in their path. They were also perpetually dirty. Butsy had cut his big toe just that morning, kicking a roofing shingle at Big Gene and Little Gene's mongrel dog. The toe was clotted over with dirt now, a sort of Mississippi band-aid. My own feet, by comparison, were tender. I enjoyed going barefoot as much as the next guy, but that pebbly asphalt in the noonday heat could raise blisters faster than a hermit crab could tuck back in his shell. But because it was dark now and the pavement had cooled down, I agreed to take off my new Keds. I left them behind the oleander and we waited for an Esso gas truck to roar past and cover our dash across the road. We reached the car and slithered under it like a couple of skinks.

They were on the seawall all right, still kissing or kissing again, you couldn't tell which. There were two cigarettes going and two bottles of beer. Everybody kept picking up bottles and passing cigarettes. Puffing, chugging, smacking. It looked unsanitary and a whole lot of fun. Eventually the boys managed to get each of the girls with a cigarette in one hand and a bottle of Goebel in the other. That left the boys' hands free to operate and the girls more or less defenseless.

I marveled at the coordination of it all. One guy was working on Louise, the other on Connie, in almost choreographed precision. They were like the swimmers in an Esther Williams movie. Backstroke, hairstroke, cheekstroke, breaststroke.

In unison, the girls responded.

"Mmmm," said Louise.

"Mmm-*mmm*," said Connie, pushing away and brushing her boy's arm with the cigarette.

"Ow. Why'dja do that fer?" her boy asked. The other pair got distracted and came up for air.

"Not *here*," said Connie. " Let's go down by the water."

"Too much sand," chimed in Louise.

"Suppose my daddy drives by," Connie insisted.

"Then let's git in the car, lak we said first-off," said Louise's boy.

"My momma said... "

"She said don't go *ridin'* anywhere," Louise pointed out, getting to her feet. "Dibs on the back seat."

The boys took last, expert drags on the cigarettes and flicked them out onto the sand, like twin shooting stars. They gave each other a knowing wink and followed the girls into the car. Connie's boy picked up what remained of a six-pack of beer and Brewster the Goebel Rooster seemed to wink, too, as he swung by my face and into the car.

The Chevy creaked and rocked. The oilpan descended onto Butsy's head and he let out a barely audible "daggone."

"Ssssh."

"Just like in the daggoone dirtyclothes. We ain't gonna see nothin."

170

Butsy was right. We heard the call for a churchkey, the sizzle of beers opening, the rushing by of occasional cars and the intermittent creak of the Chevy's leafsprings, but we couldn't see a thing.

I started crawling forward, toward the seawall. I felt Butsy's tug at my pants leg.

"Where you goin'?"

"To see."

"You gonna get us caught."

But I was out and crouched at the front fender of the Chevrolet. It was black on the bottom and white on top, with a fat chrome strip along the middle. From inside came the muffled sounds of green passion.

Pressed to the car, soundlessly, I inched upward. My warm cheek was cooled by the sliding steel. When I figured the top of my head was level with the open window I stopped and reached my hand up for the ledge of the door, found it and steadied myself. The best chance was a quick move, up and down again, like a jack-in-the-box.

I took the chance.

Up-look-down.

Then I relaxed in my crouch to consider what I'd seen. It was strictly a front-seat view. Connie was sprawled the width of the seat, back down, sort of leaning against her guy, who was pushed against the door on the driver's side. His left arm was useless, probably all pins-and-needles the way he had it, on account of the steering wheel being in the way. His right hand had all the work and it was working hard on Connie's leg, what he could reach of it. Meanwhile, he was scrunched down and she was arched back so they could kiss. It looked mighty uncomfortable.

I popped up for another look.

This time Connie's hand was pulling down her skirt and

gently pushing away his hand. The kiss was still on.

I popped up again.

He was reaching around Connie's hand and up under the skirt on her left leg. There was no letup on the kiss.

Next time I popped up, Connie had her fingers twined in his and squeezing for all she was worth, only now she had his hand six inches in the air over her hiked-up skirt. He was trying to snake his left arm through the steering wheel like a tag-team wrestler coming through the ropes, but I could tell that wouldn't work. No end in sight for the kiss.

I felt something slapping at my foot and I knew it was Butsy. So far he wasn't going to have a whole lot to report to the rest of the family.

"Daggone, you're gonna get us caught. Get back under here. What's goin' on?"

Walking like a duck, I slid along the car for a peek into the back seat. I stuck my head down to give Butsy the okay sign and waddled on. That's when I hit the nest of rockachaws.

These were no young pricklies. These were rock-hard ripe, perilous as a wading pool full of sea urchins. My duck-walk brought my left foot down flat on the whole patch, all my weight on the foot. There was nothing for it but to yell.

I jumped up yelling and hopping and pulling out rock-achaws by the handful. And it was in that brief moment of excruciating pain that I glimpsed at last the stuff of boyhood heaven: a full-grown female chest.

In the back seat, unencumbered by a steering wheel or the inhibitions of working too near home, Louise and her boy had pulled out in front of the other pair, way out. When I jumped up she jumped up. Her blouse was unbutttoned and she came right out of it.

I also saw one angry Air Force cadet.

172

Rockachaws or no rockachaws, I had to get out of there. I spun and ran down the seawall. I heard the crack of Butsy's head against the oilpan and his inevitable "daggone!" of distress. I heard shouting and swearing from the guys and shrieking from the girls. I heard car doors opening and I lit out across the highway. When I looked back they were dragging Butsy from under the car.

That was the night I lost my new black hightop Keds, for which I got no end of grief a few days later. Butsy Renard threw them over the fence, socks and all, to Big Gene's and Little Gene's dog, who most likely ate them.

None of that mattered, though. A guy could go barefoot all summer in Pass Christian, once he got his feet tough. You could manage things there that you'd never even think of in the city.

ATTENDING MARVELS

A pier's no place to say a boy can't go
when scaling its padlocked gate's child's play.
Hoisted my girl up where the sand's built high.
Swayed with her late
out past the highway lights' last reach.
Felt the worn whited planks, cracks between them,
the rain-soft splinters against our backs.
Stared at black sky,
connected dots of unborn constellations
and ("Did you see that? Right over there?"
"Just out the corner of my eye.")
gasped at the hide-and-seek of shooting stars.
Felt the black sea too, our fingers down
or toes to stir the phosphorescent dreams.
Synched our heartbeats to the slap
...and slap against the tarred pine pilings
of the metronomic moon-pulled gulf.
Breeze parted curtains, youth peeped through
and spied eternity undressed,
wondering when that age arrives
that stops the questions coming.
We only glimpsed the wisdom
of our oneness with the pier,
missed, I think, assumption's moment
in the pleasure of that fine friction:
salt-sprayed skin on salt-sprayed skin.

Yet at least we did attend the marvels,
lie alone in our black domed basilica as
the pine pipes played continuo
to the music of the spheres,
as altar candles flared and fell above
and acolyte organisms lit their million vigils below.
Sighed our prayers, heard our own confessions...
for a moment we were there.
My back yet feels the cracks between the
white weathered planks,
hair still mats with salt
as I lie in bed beside you waiting
for the questions not to come.

So the city works and plays, a great book of life, divided into two parts by the bustling thoroughfare of Canal Street — a sort of Old Testament on the north, a sort of New Testament on the south.

— Merle Thorpe, "The New New Orleans," Nation's Business, January 1927

BOURBON STREET SHOESHINE HUSTLE

Shine, mustuh? Shine?
You bruise 'em, I renews 'em.
How bout a shine?
You scuff 'em, I buff 'em.
Where you from, mistuh?
Kentucky? Yeah?
I got people in Kentucky.
How bout dat shine, Kentucky man?
Betcha I can tell you where you got dem shoes.
Oh, yeah, cause I know. Mmm-hmm.
Tell you where you got dem shoes, you let me shine 'em
* up, okay?*
Okay?
I know right where you got dem shoes.
You got 'em on yo feet.
Yeah, yeah.
Step ovuh hyanh in de shade.
I give you a shine make you blin'.
Yeah you right.

In no other city in the world do older women retain their joie de vivre , their keen interest in the passing pageant of life and their charm of manner and conversation.

— *Edward LaRoque Tinker,
Mardi Gras Masks, 1931*

CRACKING WINDOWS

If you want to know a city, ride its buses. Eavesdropping on bus converations is better than invitations to Sunday dinner. It's like tasting the ingredients before they go into the pot, so you can better comprehend the finished flavor.

But a word of caution: don't expect the same effect on streetcars. The old St. Charles line is nostalgic, romantic, and usually fun, but it's too noisy for spying. Instead, try boarding a bus near Canal Street. Heading uptown on the Magazine or Claiborne lines can be fruitful, but I prefer a downtown route. Say, the Desire or Franklin Avenue lines. The last vestiges of Creole society lie in that direction. The dialect can be difficult, but listen for that first flash of recognition between two old friends and your ears will catch on quickly.

"Mah *Gawd!*"

"Sylva-nee! Ha you *been*, dawlin'?"

"Ah been good, sugah, 'cept fo' dis aw-tu-ritis." Sylvanie, seated on the aisle, holds up both hands and flexes her gnarled knuckles. She is a tiny, hawk-nosed woman with tight black curls and thick eyeglasses.

Her friend is twice Sylvanie's size and lugs a blue-and-white shopping bag from Krauss Department Store. She heaves herself into the seat across the aisle from Sylvanie, next to a young black man whose eyes are covered by saucer-size shades and whose ears are plugged with radio earphones. The aisle between the two women creates the optimum situation for eavesdropping.

"Ha's yo' mama?" the newcomer inquires.

Sylvanie, looking too old to have a live mama, snorts. "Shenh," it sounds like. The nasal quality testifies to the French in her ancestry. She is for sure a Lapsed White Creole.

"Dat ol 'lady gon' be de deat' o' me, Marguerite. Complain, complain, complain. Ah mean she can *do* some complainin'."

"She been laid up?"

"Honey, she's strivin'. Mah mama's gonna outlive me an' you bot'. You wait an' see."

"You mean to tell me you got her livin' at home wi' chew nah?"

"*Nah?* She been wit' me since Uncle Noonootz passed."

"Noonootz? He died? He's a young man yet. Ha' it happened?"

"Backin' out 'is own drive. Ah tol' em dey oughta not let dat blin' fool drive, but ain't nobody never listen to me, no. Dey had a big red Barq's truck pulled across the drive bah de coib, too, an' t'ank Gawd de delivery man wasn't on his way up de drive wid de sof'drink cases yet or he'd a-been killed too, mos' likely."

"Noonootz nevuh seen de Barq's truck?"

"You'd a-t'ought he'd a-seen it in dat rea'view mirra, you know? But mm-mmm. He come creamin'out dat drive like he's late fo' is own funeral. Me an' Olga done swep' up sof'drink glass bah dat coib till January. An' de accident was on Armistice Day."

"You mean you got yo' sista Olga wit' you too nah?"

"Nex' doah ta Noonootz's, same as always. Dey claim de exhilerata got stuck. Shenh! Dey ain't no excuse lettin' blin' men like dat behin'a wheel, you ax me."

"Oh, Jesus, Mary, an' Joseph," Marguerite exclaimed. One lumpy paw clutched at her heart, the other fluttered in the air in front of her face. She was bug-eyed, staring at a tin watch, its stretched rubber band lost in the fleshy folds of her wrist.

"Wassamatta?" Sylvanie asked, concerned.

"Ah f'got mah cloresterol pill."

"Enh-enh-enh," cackled Sylvanie. It might have been an admonition, it might have been a wicked laugh. "You got cloresterol, girl?"

"Ah got it bad, honey. Ah betta take me dat pill quick." Marguerite dug furiously in her large red purse and came up with a brown plastic prescription bottle. She seemed on the point of tears. "Omahgawd. Ah got nuttin' to wrench it don wit'."

"Wait a minute, dawlin'," said Sylvanie, "ah got sump'n you can wrench it don wit'." She bent down and pulled a rumpled red-and-white shopping bag from under her seat.

"You mean ta tell me you still draggin' aroun' dat Chris'mas bag from Holmes'es?" I was relieved that Marguerite's attention had been drawn from the imminent cholesterol attack. Sylvanie, bent over, rummaged in her red shopping bag as only rummagers of long practice can.

"Ain' no use t'rowin it away if it ain't broke."

"Gawd, mine didn' las' t'rough Mawdigraw. I was in Woolswoit buyin' a king cake..."

"You get yo' king cake at Woolswoit instead o' McKinzie's?"

"Dey got de bes' honey, believe you me. Ah had a bottle o' Amaretta in de bottom an' it come loose an' broke all ovuh de floah. Ah like tuh died."

"Heah-ya-go."

Sylvanie extended her bony, hirsute arm.

"Doctuh Tichenor's?"

"You wrench yo' mout' out wit' it. It ain't gonna kill ya."

Reluctantly, Marguerite took the bottle and opened it.

The young black man on the seat beside her took the headset off his ears — instantly flooding the bus with the grate of Mason Ruffington: *Ah gotta git me a gypsy woman* —and said, "Dass goo' shi', la'y. Mah mama be dreen Da'Tisnuh's ev' naht."

Marguerite smiled at the young man, suspiciously. She could not understand him because he talked funny, but she did not let on. She put the pill on her tongue, the bottle to her lips and drank. The bus smashed into one of the foot-deep potholes for which New Orleans is world-renowned. Yellow antiseptic sloshed down Marguerite's expansive flowered bosom, but she seemed unaware.

"Lawd," Sylvanie exclaimed, adjusting her denture. "When dey gonna fix dem pockholes." She tapped the leg of the businessman, another black man, on her left. "You wanna crack dat winda, mistuh? It's gettin' close in heah."

Silently, the man slid open the window. He knew what the old lady meant.

Marguerite handed the Dr. Tichenor's back to Sylvanie. "It ain't so bad as ah t'ought," she said. "Kinna reminds you o' Amaretta. You could awmos' put it on ice cream."

"Somebody's berlin' crawfish," Sylvanie observed, nose in the air. The unmistakable odor was coming through the open window. This put Marguerite in mind of a burning local issue.

"Wheah you t'ink dey gonna put dat aqua-yum up at?"

"Shenh. Dey can put it in de lake fall ah care."

"Ah heah dey gonna put it in de rivuh somewheres."

"Why in Gawd's name anybody wanna pay ta go look at a lot o' fish's beyon' me, ah tell you dat. Me, ah usta woik at mah grampa's fish stoah. Come home smellin' like erstas every night. Shenh. Dey can have dat."

"Ah remembuh dat time yo' grampaw built him dat boat."

"In de basement?"

The two women laughed, Sylvanie's thin cackle rising above the stomach-shaking tee-hee of Marguerite.

"Dey had to pull don half a wall to get it out!" Marguerite said, breaking into another tee-hee spasm and clutching Sylvanie's arm across the aisle until an imposing woman with a Maison Blanche bag pushed her way through to the rear exit door. Tears were streaming down Marguerite's face like grease running from Jimmy Dean sausage patties.

Finally she composed herself enough to ask, "You like any kinna animals, den?"

"Dey can have 'em all, be awright wit' me. Nah she's afta me to git her a dog."

"Be careful, honey, or yo' mama get jus' like Doris Day."

"Long as she don' get like dat Vanna White wit all dem monkeys. You seen dat pitchuh in de papuh?"

"You mean de udduh mont' in de *Enquiruh*? Dat ain't Vanna White wid all dem monkeys, dat's *Betty* White."

"One o'dem White women. Shenh. What a stink dat mus be remembuh ol' Lady Sanamaw." She was saying the name St. Amant, I decided. "She usta have one. Ah b'lee dey call it a mammazat."

"Oh, yeah."

"Yeah. Ah mean tuh tell ya, dat mammazat usta climb all ovuh dat woman. Ol' Man Sanamaw couldn't stan' im in de flower shop."

"You remembuh how ol' Man Sanamaw usta collec' de

rent on de graves an' make all de repaihs?"

"He usta collec' de rent awright. He usta collec' from Bishop Lavalle, too. You had to watch out or dey'd sell dat tomb right out from unduh you. Dey sold some graves six, eight tahms. De day Bishop Lavalle died, ol' Man Sanamaw had 'is stroke. You tell me dey wasn't sump'n goin' on."

"Mmmm-mmm," agreed Marguerite.

"It was All Saints Day when de mammazat finally got de ol' lady. Prob'ly de crowds got it woiked up."

"Whoooo, dey usta get some crowds in dat cemetery."

"You tellin' me? It was like a picnic. De ol' coluhd women sellin' dey pralines an' canny apples an' hot dogs."

"You could buy yo' lunch an' spend de whole day in dat cemetery."

"You had to, gettin' dere early enough to put all de flowuhs on de tombs."

"A lot o' people didn't staht scrapin' an' paintin' dey tombs till dat mawnin. But us, we usta do ouhs a whole week ahead."

"Two o'clock de parish pries'd come, I remember dat."

"T'ree, it was."

"All dem altar boys."

"An' de orphan chirren, too. Double-file, all de way to dat big cross in de back."

"Dey had dat big ol' tree back dere at de en' o' de road bah dat cross. Den dey hel' de ceremonies. All dem people, dat's what got dat mammazat stahted. Screamin' an hollerin' an' goin' on. Climbed right up inside ol' Lady Sanamaw's dress an' up t'rou de bodice."

"Mmm-mmm." Marguerite shook her great head and began the heave that would lift her to her feet. "Well, de nex' stop's mahn, dawlin'. It's been good talkin' to ya."

"Yeah," said Sylvanie, "Nex' t'ing ya know dat mammazat had his teet' in dat ol' woman's eah-lobe."

Marguerite began moving away. "Tell yo' mama I said hi, awright?"

"Awright. You know she nevuh could weah no earrings aftuh dat."

"Mmm-mmm." Marguerite was at the back as the bus swayed to a stop. "You call me sometime," she said.

"Awright," Sylvanie called out, smiling and waving.

As the bus lurched off again, the little lady was rearranging the contents of her Holmes shopping bag. She lifted it into her lap and settled back into the seat. Three stops later she stood up and carefully made her way toward the front, telling the driver where she wanted to get off. I imagined her doing this every day, or perhaps on the same day each week.

The businessman placed his neatly-folded newspaper on the seat where Sylvanie had sat. He slid the window down as the bus pulled away from a street of shotgun-double houses. Half a block down, a dark figure sat hunched on a stoop. Sylvanie hoisted the Christmas bag into one arm, protected her handbag from strangers with the other, and turned down the street toward Mama.

MARSH

Flying,
And down below: the marble
Of Louisiana marsh,
A child's canvas, splotched
With number six brown,
Number eleven brown,
And twenty-two green.
Water everywhere
Eats up the scrub like
Mange on the Earth's hide
Stagnates in puddles,
Lies calm in lakes,
Over and over melts into mud,
Sometimes curves, branches, points
Like the veins of an ancient crone.

HONEY ISLAND

One of the best ways to see the land the way Bienville found it is to drive across the I-10 bridge to Slidell and spend some time in Honey Island Swamp.

Try it on a hard, clear morning in spring or under the crush of a hot August sky. Find yourself conjured to a cool and gladey place where the only noise is the laughter of great birds. The still-blue sky may tease you with torrents of sudden rain that ignore your umbrella of tupelo gum and moss-hung cypress. But even then, sitting soaked on soaked boards of a puddle-bottomed skiff, even then you'll find yourself laughing, loud as those lurid birds, laughing at yourself for waiting so long to come here.

Feel your eyes fill with rain and wonder and know the joke's on all of us who've never fallen in love with this swamp.

It's always been here, almost in sight of the city, alive with gators and black bears and even Florida panthers. It teems with tales of outlaws and pirates and broods with the mystery of the Honey Island Swamp Monster. It was just this way from the beginning, before the Colapissa Indians piled their clamshell mounds and studied the ways of the osprey. Today more than a million humans live on its fringes. Spaceship engines boom and roar at the Mississippi Test Facility next door and the Interstate cuts across its middle, but few of us ever venture into the most forbidding and pristine swamp in North America.

The Pearl River's the source of the swamp. Snaking down from Jackson, the Pearl holds itself together until it crosses the line into Louisiana. Just past Bogalusa the river divides into several channels. Near Slidell, the channels split again, like arteries becoming veins, and the water forms first a swamp, then a marsh, before it merges into the salty Gulf of Mexico. It was just at the upper fringe of the marsh that a French trapper discovered a ridge of solid ground, swarming with honeybees. He called the ridge "Honey Island" and the swamp took its name from there.

In the 19th century the swamp provided a fine refuge for some of the pirates who worked the gulf shipping lanes. Pierre Rameau was the Pirate King of Honey Island Swamp. This Rameau had a different name in New Orleans where he posed as a respectable businessman. They say Rameau bore no love for that other pirate king, Jean Lafitte, and when Lafitte went to the aid of General Jackson in the Battle of New Orleans, Rameau and his men signed up with the British. Legend has it he died in that battle, but his ghost still guards his booty, buried deep in the swamp.

Half a century later, a band of cutthroats called the Copeland Gang terrorized Mississippi and hid out across the state line in the swamp. Between their buried treasure and the pirates', it's a wonder there's any room left in Honey Island for the Swamp Monster. But too many folks have seen that creature to deny it a place. One fellow's even made casts of its footprints.

Toward the end of the last century, some farmers staked their claim to the fertile soil around the swamp's edges. For a few years there was livestock grazing among the cypress knees and duckweed. Then the great hurricane of 1900 came and wiped out the farmers and most of their animals. Only the swine survived. The hogs went back to the wild, evolution in rapid reverse. Today they roam the swamp in surly packs, hair growing thicker and tusks longer. You rarely catch sight of them, but you can hear them grunting and squealing and crashing through the cane, the most dangerous thing in the swamp next to weekend hunters. And the Monster.

Civilization, such as we know it, ends today at Indian Village Landing on the banks of the West Pearl River. There's a boat launch there, littered with Pepsi bottles and Bud cans, the droppings of those fishermen who must mark their territory like dogs. Across the still, black water is a cluster of fishing camps on rickety stilts. Some are painted, some not. Doors are whimsically hung and window ledges are crammed with rusting gear. A single electric line, like a dead vine, creeps from camp to camp, tree to tree. Where the electricity ends, the shock of utter solitude begins. You are alone with the earth.

Ahead lies the wide-domed beaver lodge. Beside it, acres of tall wild rice, golden green in the late sun, filling Lower Dead Lake like a Kansas wheatfield. A fat, bottle-shaped duck rises from the rice and flaps south. A wood duck. The wild rice is their favorite food.

The water about seems still, but it is in constant motion, keeping Honey Island as pure and untouched a bottomland hardwood swamp as there is anywhere. A swamp needs its yearly flood, to spread water over the basin and renew the land. The animals breed then and the fish spawn. When the water lowers again it leaves behind mudbanks where the cypress cones can germinate.

The flushing streams afford little refuge for mosquitoes. The constant exchange between air and water cools the swamp. Consequently, even in August, Honey Island Swamp can be an eerily inviting place.

Turning from the main river, you enter a bayou. Turning again, into a smaller branch, you will be in a slough ("sloo"), which dead ends in the deepest swamp, impass-able. The heart of nowhere. In the distance there is a shrill call, like a high-pitched bullroarer. The swamp monster?

Honey Island is the swamp chosen by the Walt Disney people for their nature movie at Epcot. They found out there is nothing quite so wild as this in the Everglades. Don't wait for the movie, though. See it for yourself.

You might see a wild hog. You might see a diamond-back rattler coiled on the bank, swallowing a catfish whole. You might see a great blue heron defy gravity with the slow beat of its impossible wings. You might see an anhinga, a water turkey, snaking through the air like a pterodactyl. Go in the spring and you might even see this year's pair of bald eaglets lift off from their White Kitchen aerie, learning to soar and hunt.

You will see a splendid, tangled collection of plant life. Splayfooted tupelo gum and black gum, alongside the deep-canyoned bald cypress. Ash trees draped over a slough, leaning on each other's shoulders like drunken sentinels. Swamp bays, matted roots undercut by the bayou to make them seem suspended from the banks. Titis, with small pale berries on red stems. Irises, marsh asters, swamp lilies, and spider lilies. Duck potatoes, leaves as large as elephant ears, with underwater tubers the Indians used to eat.

After a summer shower the mist hangs like golden pollen over the duckweed and water hyacinth. The wild rice and the cut grass seem to glow in the sudden release of light. Curve-billed ibises stretch their wings and shake off the raindrops, and lift languidly from their storm-perches. It's then you feel God himself might be waiting at the end of the next slough. It's then you understand the need you'll feel to come here again.

CRESCENT CITY

From a bowed decomposing bed
the violated swamp hove her half-caste child
at droning, contentious poor surrounds,
left her cleft to the brown river
that speeds by heedless of the moment
and to the sere transpired past.

Doomed to awe antiquity
where even cypress giants' roots court rejection,
she fed on borrowed bread, paved
sinking streets with ballast stones
thieved like her music from the Old World.
She drowned sorrows, minted dreams.

Aching, arched now, tumescent,
the crescent pounds against tomorrow, slow to mate
as the elephant, worldly wise,
double sexed as half her sons
and daughters, puritan procurer-
princess of the New World's waste.

From her pleasure palace cries,
"It's here, here between my thighs beauty lies."
Quartermoon octoroon,
silver-spoon city soon,
wall yourself in mirrors, wait
in your bowed bed by the leering river.

The river is the sole enemy to be dreaded, but a terrible one; it is gnawing the levee to get at the fat canefields; it is devouring the roadway; it is burrowing nearer and nearer to the groves and the gardens.

— *Lafcadio Hearn,*
  "The Scenes of Cable's Romances,"
  Century Magazine, 1883

The greatest friend and the greatest enemy of New Orleans has always been the Mississippi River.

— *Lyle Saxon,*
  Fabulous Old New Orleans, 1928

Report Call to Wife

uicide Victim' Still Aliv

By ROSS YOCKEY

A man who left a suicide note in his
Long Bridge Oct. 13 may never have ta
States-Item learned today.

An investigation revealed that the Jeff
staff feels that Everett Lee Ingalls is w

A spokesman for the sher-
iff's office, who asked not to
be identified, said th
wife informed
she ha

ISSING MAN'S

Bridge Leap Is Thwarted

Woman's Jump Halte By Passer

uicide n
his wife, S
The brief
"My Dear
thing I've tr
solve the situ
been to no a
allow you and
suffer further b
There is nothing

"I'm sorry it hi   ns
way. I love you, Sandy. I love
the children. I love you.—
Lee."

The note also mentioned the
name of a   hom Ingalls   money.
nation"
se of

sher-
phy-
ene
at

tive for t
tive Agen
fore the
had gone
and Vinso
tors.

INGALL
to comm
telephone

Mrs. S
their thre
6, have le
at the Vic
They h
Ingalls' p
Evrett L.
land, Algi
A repo
family ye
Sec

GOIN' TO THE RIVER

The Mississippi River, if it had its way, would drop us in a minute and head west. The river yearns to make its bed in the Atchafalaya Basin. It takes the entire U. S. Army Corps of Engineers to keep it in its place.

The Corps' system of levees, floodgates, spillways, and jetties that bends the Mississippi to our will just might be the most ambitious engineering project in mankind's short history. Still, it would take no more than a runaway barge in spring flood to change the river's course and leave New Orleans low and dry. It happened to the Tigris and the Euphrates. It could happen here.

While we've got her still, go and watch the river. The ferry boat's a good place because you can stand on the deck and feel the pulse of her current in mid-stream. You can cut across the bows of rusty inbound tankers, rock in the wakes of coal-barge strings and grain ships heading out. Another good thing's to stand in the soggy grass of the batture beneath a willow and feel puny next to the breadth and character of that single stream.

The river's color is relentless. This brown-gray liquid mud is a bile that dissolves any other color we dump into it. This is the ultimate hue of earth, the color all things were and all must become. Bowel and bloodstream both, this dun-colored river is finality and infinity together.

Fats Domino sang:

I'm goin' to the river, gonna jump overboard and drown,
Because the gal I love, she just has left this town.

Fats Domino is alive and well and singing still. My friend

Howard Stone, on the other hand, took the river into the next world. Nobody knows why.

Howie had two fine kids and a caring wife. He was respected in his profession. Easter Sunday night he drove the Pontchartrain Expressway to the Greater New Orleans Mississippi River Bridge. He stopped his car and got out. They still haven't found his body.

The crazy thing is, Howie loved a good time. He built a big house with a pool so he could throw parties. He belonged to two or three carnival organizations. He had his kids in good private schools, and he enjoyed pitching in on committees. They probably would have put him on the school board next year. You could count on Howie to take the edge off serious moments with a wisecrack.

He wasn't at his funeral, but they held the service anyway. Mrs. Stone, Shirley, sat in the front pew, refusing to cry. His boys served on the altar, busy with their cruets and their bells. The Irish priest talked about God's will. I wondered what the hell had happened to Howie's will. Since it's no use getting mad at God, I got mad at Howie, like his wife was, like his boys will be later.

The rest of us in church that morning, we're all so much like Howie, with our big houses and our good jobs and our private schools. It could have been any of us. Why was it Howie in the river? Were his private agonies that much worse than any of ours? I wanted to talk long and hard to Howie, like I'd never talked with him before.

My first job out of college was news reporting for the old *States-Item*. One of my earliest "investigative" stories was about a man who left a suicide note in his car on the same bridge, right about where Howie must have parked his car. The police were suspicious that maybe this other guy wasn't really a suicide at all. They suspected he was still alive, so they had his wife's phone tapped.

I went to Algiers, on the West Bank, to interview the widow-slash-accomplish. She had a nice house in a quiet neighborhood. She seemed suitably bereaved and cried real tears. She loaned me a snapshot of the two of them on the beach in Waveland. Something was wrong.

I was trying to figure out what bothered me about this suicide, riding back to the city in a taxicab, when I noticed the driver swerving around a parked car, stopped in the middle of the bridge. The driver muttered a curse and I looked out of the window. A woman was walking from the car to the railing and I knew she was going to jump.

By the time I got the driver to stop, we'd gone a hundred yards or more. I hit the bridge pavement running, but didn't think I'd reach her in time. I could see she was a small woman in an average sort of dress, average hair blown about her face by an average wind. I shouted and the word "wait" came out. Wait for what, wait until when? She appeared not to hear me. She climbed the railing, swung her legs over and sat on the steel. She was not looking down but straight ahead. There was a screech of brakes and a blowing of horns. Another man was running toward her. She looked over her shoulder and saw the man. Then she leaned forward and stared for the first time at the brown-gray water half a mile below. Her fingers began to slide along the rail. We lunged, the other man and I, caught her arms together as they came off the rail. She was falling when we got her.

Together we pulled her to what we considered safety. I thought she would scream, but she was silent, staring as before. She collapsed on the hot pavement that quivered and wagged from the passing traffic. Then she looked at me, into me. Her eyes were filled with deep anger, the rage of one whose questions have not been answered.

It is rage these jumpers feel, something beyond despair, and it is rage they leave behind as a legacy to the rest of us. I realized then there had been none of this anger in the eyes of the woman whose husband was supposed to have committed suicide. As it turned out, he was alive and in California, waiting for his creditors to write him off, waiting for his wife to sell the house and move out there to join him.

The Louisiana novelist Walker Percy pondered suicide in his book *Lost in the Cosmos.* He decided that contemplating and rejecting suicide builds character. You're a better person, Percy thinks, for examining escape as an alternative and then turning your back on it to reaffirm life, free of anxiety. Maybe.

I heard a fine sermon preached on that point by Dr. Kenneth Phifer at St. Charles Avenue Presbyterian Church. His text that Sunday was from the Book of Job.

Job stood "out at the naked edge of the world," said the preacher, quoting Thomas Wolfe, "staring into the abyss, yearning to die...until he discovers he can live without having his questions answered."

Only at that point, he said, did Job "take up with people again, as though Job had to re-enter the human community before he could start picking up the pieces of his life again. You cannot put life together without other people."

And that's the point my friend Howie Stone never reached. If he'd given other people half a chance, they'd have helped him sort out the jumbled pieces of his life. But Howie figured his questions were the only questions in the world that couldn't be answered. He never got to Job's position, or Walker Percy's, of turning his back on suicide. Thank goodness most of us never go as far along that path as Howie went. Most of us just put the questions out of our mind, if we ever even ask them.

New Orleans, better than any other society of my acquaintance, makes it possible for people to go through life without ever knowing those questions are there. Or, if they nag us now and then, the city shows us wonderful distractions.

Our history here provides a fatalistic sense of destiny, even of eternity. Our religion makes salvation a birthright, convenient, and on call. Our preoccupation with pleasure provides an insulation we perceive as purpose. We don't mind a little exploitation because the tourists pay to share our good times. Our elected leaders, by deed and example, reaffirm our commitment to an almost-free ride.

If only it weren't for our river and our canals and bayous, we wouldn't need all those bridges. Maybe we should get rid of them. You never hear of folks killing themselves by jumping off the Jackson Avenue Ferry.

We have a fable that whoever drinks of the Mississippi River water while in this old town is bound to come again; so we hope you will drink some — filtered — and that you will return, and that then we will have still more evidence of progress and happiness to show you.

— Around the St. Charles Belt
New Orleans and Carrollton Railroad,
Light and Power Company, 1901

ACKNOWLEDGEMENTS
AND
AFTERTHOUGHTS

This book owes its life to a great many people who can never be thanked. Among those who can is my wife, Joann, who typed and retyped, planned and guided every step of the way. Relatives and friends gave advice, encouragement, and materials. Carol and Jim Scott provided art and illustrations. Shirley Bowler edited and proofread. Myldred Masson Costa allowed inclusion of segments of her book. *Louisiana Life, New Orleans Magazine* and *WYES-TV* gave permission to include materials which first appeared there. My mother understood. I thank them one and all.

One parting word about the Creole Songs. It would be gratifying to say that these verses are faithful translations of the original. But the truth is that only the merest fragments of this astonishing folk literature have survived. Of the lyrics and music available to the present generation in published form, most are so tainted and expurgated as to cast only the faintest shadows of the life they celebrate. Our restoration project of the past ten years has resulted in what must be read as "original work." Yet our only goal has been to scrape away the pentimento of all the intervening generations, to convey at least a memory of what must have been.